Letter from the Editor

Dear Readers,

We are very excited to welcome you all to the sixth volume of The Arbitration Brief. The Arbitration Brief is a student publication of the American University Washington College of Law. The Arbitration Brief aims to become a leading academic publication for arbitration-related matters in the United States and abroad.

The Arbitration Brief is an entirely student-run organization. We publish articles submitted by professors, arbitrators, practitioners, and students alike. All articles are selected, edited, and published by the Brief's editorial board and staff.

The Arbitration Brief would like to thank the authors of this issue for their patience, responsiveness, and cooperation with our editorial board as we revised their articles. The Arbitration Brief would also like to thank Professor Horacio Grigera- Naón, Dr. Björn Arp, Susana Castiglione, and Adam Briscoe for their continuous support and encouragement. The Arbitration Brief would like to express its deep gratitude to the International Center on Commercial Arbitration, without whom this publication would not have been possible. Finally, I would like to personally thank the Brief's staff for their exceptional editing and tireless work ethic that has culminated in this issue.

Please explore our website for more information about The Arbitration Brief. If you have any questions, please feel free to reach out to arbitrationbrief@wcl.american.edu.

Best Regards,
Michelle Avrutin
Editor-in-Chief
Volume 6

THE ARBITRATION BRIEF

Volume 6

The Arbitration Brief is a student publication of American University Washington College of Law prepared with the assistance of the Washington College of Law Center on International Commercial Arbitration. The mission of this publication is to provide timely information, both practical and academic, on developments in the field of arbitration. We welcome pieces from academics, practicing attorneys, arbitrators, and students. For more information, please contact arbitrationbrief@wcl.american.edu. The views expressed in this publication are those of the writers and are not necessarily those of the editors, the Center on International Commercial Arbitration, or American University.

THE ARBITRATION BRIEF STAFF 2019-2020

EDITOR-IN-CHIEF
Michelle Avrutin

MANAGING EDITOR
Leslie Castello

SENIOR ARTICLES EDITORS
Elena Zhilinskaya
Gaensly Joseph

ARTICLES EDITORS
Sabrina Espinal
Marcel Apple
Charles Frazer
Amy Allen
Hannah Stephens
Susan Farhang

Table of Contents

Conference Report: Handling Allegations of Corruption in Arbitration and Judicial Dispute Settlement *1*

Arbitrators' Authority: Scope and Limitations *12*

The Investor-State Dispute Settlement System Amidst Crisis, Collapse, and Reform *20*

When Peer Pressure is Not Enough: Mandatory Disclosure and Third-Party Funding *60*

CONFERENCE REPORT:
HANDLING ALLEGATIONS OF CORRUPTION IN ARBITRATION AND
JUDICIAL DISPUTE SETTLEMENT

Björn Arp[*] and *Adam Briscoe*[**]

I. Introduction

On February 18, 2019, the Center on International Commercial Arbitration[1] (Arbitration Center) and the U.S. & International Anti-Corruption Law Program[2] (Anti-Corruption Program) co-sponsored a panel titled "Handling Allegations of Corruption in Arbitration and Judicial Dispute Resolution" at American University Washington College of Law (AUWCL). It was the first time the Arbitration Center joined forces with the Anti-Corruption Program to provide expert analysis on the cross-cutting issue of corruption. Thanks to this cooperation, it was possible to bring together an interdisciplinary panel of expert practitioners, including a U.S. district court judge, academics, and arbitration practitioners to explore corruption issues in both international arbitration and domestic litigation and postulate the consequences that such issues can have across diverse legal fields, the economy, and government.

AUWCL Professor Susan Franck opened the event by stating that the panel occurs at a time when the world is witnessing a sharp rise in nationalist sentiment and a "resurgence" in calls for the removal from international legal bodies. Franck acknowledged however, that at the same time, there are increased calls for active arbitral tribunals and judiciaries to parse out the issues in resolving disputes containing allegations of corruption. Examples Professor

---

[*] Adjunct Faculty and Fellow, Center on International Commercial Arbitration, and Assistant Director for International Curriculum Development, International and Comparative Legal Studies, at American University Washington College of Law. For any comments, please contact arp@american.edu.

[**] Law Clerk, Wiley Rein LLP. Editor-in-Chief of the Arbitration Brief, 2017-19.

[1] For more information on the Center on International Commercial Arbitration, see online at www.wcl.american/arbitration.

[2] For more information on the U.S. & International Anti-Corruption Law Program, see online at www.wcl.american/anti-corruption.

Franck pointed out include the EU proposal for an investment court, calls for an international court of civil justice, and an international corruption court. Quoting a World Bank study that found corruption costs the world economy about $2 trillion per year,[3] Professor Franck acknowledged that corruption still maintains a stronghold in international economics. Franck concluded that because of these ongoing developments, this panel's exploration of complex corruption issues that arise out of international economic law is both timely and relevant.

Nancy Boswell, Director of the US and International Anti-Corruption Law Certificate Program and Adjunct Professor at AUWCL, moderated the panel. In her introductory remarks, Boswell underlined the "central importance" of corruption as an issue that may arise in both arbitration and domestic court proceedings. She pointed out that corruption affects not only the business community, but also environmental and human rights protection efforts.

Boswell continued by taking stock of where the international community currently finds itself in relation to handling allegations of corruption. She emphasized that achieving international consensus on issues of corruption remains a key challenge. Although there is still no universal definition for corruption, Boswell commented that international consensus has been reached on the fact that corruption is harmful, wrong, and an unacceptable cost to pay. She stated that consensus has also been reached in legal regimes, citing the OECD Convention on Combating Bribery of Foreign Public Officials in International Business Transactions,[4] Inter-American Convention Against Corruption,[5] and the UN

---

[3] To illustrate this point, the United Nations (U.N.) Secretary General António Guterres stated on the International Anti-Corruption Day on December 9, 2018, that the World Economic Forum estimates the global cost of corruption is at least $2.6 trillion, or 5 percent of the global gross domestic product (GDP). He further indicated that according to the World Bank, businesses and individuals pay more than $1 trillion in bribes every year. See *Secretary-General's Message for 2018*, available online at
https://www.un.org/en/events/anticorruptionday/messages.shtml.
[4] Adopted on December 17, 1997, *U.N.T.S.* vol. 2802, I-49274.
[5] Adopted on March 29, 1996, *OAS Series* B-58.

Convention Against Corruption[6] as prime examples. Although none of these conventions explicitly define corruption, Boswell noted that these conventions do enumerate criminal acts, which include active and passive bribery.

Despite these hard-fought developments, Boswell made it clear that the anti-corruption field is a work in progress, highlighted by the significant cultural differences among nations with respect to corruption. She called attention to these differences when looking at some of the provisions of the Foreign Corrupt Practices Act (FCPA).[7] While this legislation contains an exception for facilitation payments, such payments might be viewed as bribes in other countries or regions of the world. Additionally, while the FCPA prohibits giving gifts to foreign officials, this may be seen as customary in other cultures. Boswell concluded that these cultural differences and approaches to corruption are particularly important when such an allegation arises before a court or arbitral tribunal.

II. Cross-Cutting Issues of Corruption in Judicial and Arbitral Dispute Settlement

Lucinda Low, Partner at Steptoe & Johnson LLP, began her remarks by putting the discussion about corruption into the context of the intersection between white-collar crime and international arbitration. In tracing the development of international standards and national laws on corruption, Low opined that the process began with the concept of criminalization. This process included the criminalization of various acts of corruption, provided infrastructure for cooperation among countries in corruption investigations, and established some limited preventative measures.

Low then noted that criminalization prompted an increase in enforcement activities by national governments for those who have political will and capacity to investigate. She commented that multi-jurisdictional cases are increasing because multiple countries can have jurisdiction over the same criminal conduct, as long as

---

[6] Adopted on October 31, 2003, U.N. Doc. A/58/422; *U.N.T.S.*, vol. 2349, p. 41.
[7] Foreign Corrupt Practices Act of 1977, 15 U.S.C. § 78dd-1, et seq.

the crime crossed national borders. This has led to a spillover effect, where some civil cases that included allegations of corruption have prompted criminal prosecutions under national law. Low highlighted this stage of development by the *Aluminum Bahrain B.S.C. (Alba) v. Alcoa, Inc.* case. In this case, Alba, an Alcoa customer, sued Alcoa in the United States claiming that the contracts they entered into were tainted by corruption and sought damages. The civil case led to a criminal prosecution and Alcoa ultimately paid substantial fines.[8]

Low noted that in a majority of international disputes, arbitration is a more popular form of dispute resolution than litigation. In recent years, she commented that there has been a large increase in corruption allegations arising in both commercial and investor-state arbitration disputes. One case that will play out over the coming years and led to new developments in the prevention and sanctioning of corruption is the Brazilian *Odebrecht* case.

Low explained that the corruption issue is typically asserted as a defense in arbitration. In commercial arbitration, it may be an agent suing for money under an agency contract and the respondent's defense is that the agent acted corruptly, or that the contract was procured by corruption. In the investor-state context, Low noted that typically the state claims that the investment was either procured through corruption or performed in a corrupt manner. If the investment treaty requires that the investment be made in accordance with the local law, these state claims raise issues of jurisdiction. Otherwise, Low explained, the corruption defense raises issues of claim admissibility and the question for the tribunal to decide becomes whether corruption is a concept of international public policy. Low noted that sometimes the tribunal raises the issue of corruption by itself. The possibility of *sua sponte* action by the tribunal depends on the powers and duties of

---

[8] See Department of Justice Press Release, *Alcoa World Alumina Agrees to Plead Guilty to Foreign Bribery and Pay $223 Million in Fines and Forfeiture*, January 9, 2014, available online at https://star.worldbank.org/corruption-cases/sites/corruption-cases/files/ALBA_Alcoa_US_DOJ_SEC_Settlement_PR_Jan_9_2014.pdf.

arbitrators. In fact, Low indicated that arbitrators may be at risk if they do not further investigate "red flags", or indicators of corruption.

Low then discussed how issues of proof are central to dealing with corruption allegations in arbitration. When corruption allegations are raised in arbitration, and the home or host government has done no investigation, the tribunal is left to its own fact-finding resources. In these circumstances, Low commented that there are big debates among parties and institutions as to what the burden or standards of proof are to prove corruption. These are some unanswered and contentious questions that Low stressed are key for the legal community to work out in the coming years.

When a tribunal reaches a finding of corruption, Low stated that the tribunal must determine the consequences of this wrongdoing. An example of the consequences for a finding of corruption may be the dismissal of the claim for lack of jurisdiction, even if the party performed under the contract, or the state received benefits under the contract. Low noted that the key case that dealt with findings of corruption is *World Duty Free v. Kenya*.[9] In this investor-state case, a principal shareholder of the claimant submitted an affidavit admitting that he paid a bribe to the President of Kenya. The principal shareholder claimed that it was a customary payment for doing business in the country. The tribunal concluded that paying the bribe violated public policy and dismissed the claim. Strikingly, Low mentioned that the tribunal refused to attribute the conduct of the President of Kenya to the state, and as a result, Kenya got to keep benefits conferred under the contract by World Duty Free until that point in time. This decision was highly controversial and left arbitrators, practitioners, and academics wondering what the consequences should be in such cases. Low concluded her comments by highlighting that because states now perceive corruption defenses to be a "get-out-of-jail-free-card," states will lodge aggressive investigations into investor companies when there are legal disputes in order to build a corruption defense that can defeat an arbitration claim.

---

[9] *World Duty Free Co. Ltd. v. Republic of Kenya*, ICSID Case No. ARB/00/7, Award of October 4, 2006.

III. Corruption and the Judiciary

The Honorable Judge Carlos Acosta, an Associate Justice at the United States District Court for the District of Maryland, began his discussion of corruption allegations before U.S. courts with a reference to a U.S. Senate Report which stated that when bribes are paid, contracts don't go to the most efficient producer but to the most corrupt. For these reasons, Judge Acosta stated that enforcing anti-corruption measures is sound public policy that also protects taxpayers.

Discussing the history of the FCPA, Judge Acosta mentioned that some of the key reasons why this legislation was passed was due to cases of foreign bribery by Lockheed Martin and Chiquita. These cases gave rise to public uncertainty and dissatisfaction in the conduct of U.S. public companies doing business abroad, and ultimately led to the passage of the FCPA in 1977. Explaining the two central prongs of the FCPA, transparency of securities and bribery of foreign officials, Judge Acosta narrowed the scope of his comments to the latter. Judge Acosta pointed out that when looking at the regulation of bribery of foreign officials under the FCPA, the law does not ban facilitation payments, otherwise known as "greasing the wheel" payments. He stressed that although the FCPA may not prohibit these forms of payments, national laws may, and so any U.S. business or individual doing business abroad should be very cognizant of the legal regime that they are working under.

Delving into some major cases under the FCPA, Judge Acosta highlighted the 2008 Siemens AG case, which resulted in a $450 million fine.[10] He also noted the 2012 Marubeni Corporation FCPA violation, which resulted in a $54 million fine for acting as an agent for a joint venture in Nigeria, where the corporation paid $51 million in bribes to Nigerian officials.[11] Judge Acosta noted

---

[10] *See SEC Charges Siemens AG for Engaging in Worldwide Bribery*, Press Release No. 2008-294, SEC Docket, (2008), available online at https://www.sec.gov/news/press/2008/2008-294.htm.
[11] *See Marubeni Corporation Resolves Foreign Corrupt Practices Act Investigation and Agrees to Pay a $54.6 Million Criminal Penalty*, Press Release No. 12-060, Dep't of Just. Docket (2012), available online at

that courts do not often hold formal trials in these cases. Instead, the suspect companies are offered deferred prosecution agreements in order to talk, pay a substantial fine, and ultimately avoid jail time. Reflecting on his time as a prosecutor, Judge Acosta stated that the difficulty in FCPA cases is proving the corrupt conduct or scheme.

Turning to a major government procurement corruption case, Judge Acosta discussed the Fat Leonard scandal. This scandal involved Leonard Glen Francis, a Malaysian national, and his company Glen Defense Marine Asia, which supplied U.S. Navy ships with rations, supplies, and services when they came into ports across the Pacific Rim region. In order to win these resupply contracts, Francis bribed high-ranking members of the U.S. Navy with vacations, shows, prostitutes, cigars, and cash payments. More than 550 members of the U.S. Navy were investigated in this scandal, 33 of whom were prosecuted.[12] Judge Acosta alluded to how the Fat Leonard scandal and other cases in the federal procurement arena highlighted major areas of fraud in government procurement work. These areas include violations of the Buy American Act, unmet labor standards, overbilling, double-billing, price gouging, counterfeit products, and kickback schemes.[13] Judge Acosta concluded that the U.S. government fortunately has the resources to investigate when there is a complaint of wrongdoing in the U.S., which ultimately leads to court proceedings and convictions under the U.S. anti-corruption legal regime.

IV. Corruption Allegations in International Arbitration

The third speaker, Aloysius (Louie) Llamzon, a Senior Associate in the International Arbitration group at King & Spalding LLP, began by noting that it is alarming to both

---

https://www.justice.gov/opa/pr/marubeni-corporation-resolves-foreign-corrupt-practices-act-investigation-and-agrees-pay-546.

[12] *See* Craig Whitlock & Kevin Uhrmacher, *Prostitutes, Vacations and Cash: The Navy Officials 'Fat Leonard' Took Down*, Wash. Post, Sept. 20, 2018, available online at
https://www.washingtonpost.com/graphics/investigations/seducing-the-seventh-fleet/.

[13] Buy American Act, 41 U.S.C. §§ 8301–8303 (2012).

arbitrators and practitioners when corruption is alleged, or even when the issue of corruption is raised in international arbitration cases. Llamzon traced some of the history of corruption in international arbitration and commented that it has been an issue in this field since the 1960s. Despite this, the first landmark case that addressed corruption in international arbitration, *World Duty Free Ltd. v. Kenya*, was not concluded until 2006.[14]

Llamzon discussed the differences between investment and commercial arbitration in relation to a finding of corruption and noted that the investor-state arbitration system was designed in part to minimize global corruption forces. However, Llamzon highlighted an interesting aspect of how this dynamic has unfolded over the years when he pointed out that states assert corruption defenses against investors for conduct in which public officials are equally complicit more than two-thirds of the time. Distinguishing commercial arbitration corruption cases, Llamzon noted that most of these cases arise out of "contracts for corruption" that take the form of agency agreements between a seller and an agent who helps to secure a contract for the seller by peddling insider influence. When the agency contract is not fully performed or upheld, these contracts are sent to arbitration. A second, less common type of commercial arbitration corruption case is the type of case where corruption taints the consent of a party. Llamzon noted that these cases are similar to common law cases of contractual fraud.

Llamzon next questioned whether there are real differences between the consequences of investor-state and commercial arbitration corruption cases. He started by noting that corruption can be seen as an issue of jurisdiction, admissibility, or the merits in the investor-state context. However, Llamzon noted an interesting caveat related to state responsibility in investor-state corruption cases: in such cases, a finding of corrupt conduct by a public official, or even a head of state, is not attributed to the state

---

[14] *World Duty Free Co. Ltd. v. Rep. of Kenya*, ICSID Case No. ARB/00/7, Agreement for the construction, maintenance, and operation of duty-free complexes at Nairobi and Mombasa International Airports (Oct. 4, 2006), available online at https://www.italaw.com/documents/WDFv.KenyaAward.pdf.

itself. In the commercial context, on the other hand, Llamzon explained that the contract is usually voidable or void ab initio as a principle of public policy because such a case is examined through the lens of national law. Yet even in such circumstances where the contract is voidable or void ab initio, the seller may be able to obtain non-contractual remedies for the cost of the goods they sold or other minor costs they incurred.

Llamzon concluded with a discussion on the impact of domestic proceedings connected to arbitral decisions in which he considered two distinct corruption situations. In the first situation, which is similar to *Siemens v. Argentina*, an investor wins an award and later pleads guilty in a national investigation of corrupt conduct related to the same contract, after which the investor is obligated to withdraw their acceptance of the arbitration award.[15] In the second situation, which is similar to *Niko Resources Ltd. v. Bangl. Petroleum Expl. & Prod. Co. Ltd.*, the arbitral tribunal takes a more nuanced view of corruption. In this situation, the tribunal holds that even if an investor pleads guilty in national courts to engaging in corrupt conduct while securing a contract, the corruption must taint the investment itself through an element of causation for the guilty party to be forced to relinquish all claims to an arbitration award.[16] If the opposing party cannot prove that causation connects the corrupt conduct to the investment, the arbitration can proceed.

V. Proving Corruption: The Role of Financial Experts

The final speaker of the panel, Boris Steffen, the Senior Managing Director of GlassRatner Advisory & Capital Group, discussed the roles and responsibilities that financial experts have responding to corruption allegations and conducting relevant

---

[15] *Siemens v. Argentine Republic*, ICSID Case No. ARB/02/8, Termination of a contract for Siemens to implement an immigration control, personal identification, and electoral information system, including national identity cards (Jan. 17, 2007), available online at https://www.italaw.com/sites/default/files/case-documents/ita0790.pdf.
[16] *Niko Res. Ltd. v. Bangl. Petroleum Expl. & Prod. Co. Ltd.*, ICSID Case No. ARB/10/18, Gas purchase and sale agreement, available online at https://icsid.worldbank.org/en/Pages/cases/casedetail.aspx?CaseNo=ARB%2f10%2f18.

investigations. Steffen first touched on the role of a financial expert in these cases, noting that financial experts must refute allegations of fraud by using their auditing and accounting skills to establish fact patterns and relationships. Steffen stated that there is a clear red line in the role of such experts, cautioning that it is outside of a financial expert's role—and potentially an ethical violation—to draw any conclusions regarding the existence of fraud. Such conclusions require legal interpretation, and therefore are outside of financial experts' realm of expertise.

Steffen then examined the three methods that financial experts use to collect evidence. The first is data mining, whereby the experts electronically review large data sets comprised of emails, ledgers, and other documents to determine relationships between individuals and other pertinent facts about the case. Steffen explained that the second method of evidence collection is an analysis of financial statements, which financial experts use to highlight unexpected or unanticipated financial relationships between assets and liabilities, sales forecasts, and costs. The third method of collecting evidence is by refining the scope of the investigation. Steffen noted the equal importance of interviews when conducting such investigations and stated that strategic interview methodology begins with interviews of third parties who could have pertinent knowledge regarding the facts at issue. After financial experts complete the third-party interviews, they interview any suspected parties followed by direct actors in the dispute.

Steffen explained that financial experts typically disclose "badges of fraud" or "red flags" that are indicative of fraud when reporting or testifying regarding the investigation. Examples of such red flags include unsupported expense reimbursements for charges that occurred around the time that a contract was awarded, or contracts that were awarded to a consultant whose expertise was not consistent with the contract requirements.

Steffen then listed the three methodologies that financial experts use when attempting to trace or recover assets, which include turning an inside witness, executing a covert sting operation, or conducting an asset-tracing operation using auditing methods. Steffen explained that, depending on whether the corruption scheme is classified as an illicit (on-book) or undisclosed (off-book) scheme, some of these methodologies may be preferred over others.

Steffen ended by commenting on the difference between conducting an investigation in an arbitration setting or in a judicial proceeding. In arbitration cases where an interested individual or entity is not party to the arbitration agreement, financial experts may have to deal with issues that arise regarding safeguarding assets and proving claims. Such issues may require a party to use only information within their possession to prove a claim if a tribunal views an investigation into evidence of alleged corrupt conduct to be outside the scope of the underlying arbitral dispute. In order to safeguard assets, the interested party may have to go outside four corners of the arbitral proceedings and request that a national court freeze the assets. This could alert the opposing party to the corruption allegation and lead to the sale or disposition of the relevant assets.

VI. Conclusions

Nancy Boswell concluded the panel by noting that there is currently some consensus on the harm that corruption causes, the need to do something about it, and the relevant legal framework. However, Boswell stated that we are still in the early stages of standardizing the enforcement mechanisms of corruption actions, both in national courts and in international arbitral tribunals. For these reasons, Boswell noted that it is crucial to continue discussing corruption in international arbitration. In time, this will allow us to work out the modern issues that practitioners face while also bringing new ideas to the table regarding how to generate more widely accepted anti-corruption practices throughout the legal profession.

ICC INSTITUTE OF WORLD BUSINESS LAW
THE CONDUCT OF THE PROCEEDINGS AND CASE MANAGEMENT:
THE ARBITRATOR'S PERSPECTIVE
NEW YORK, N.Y. 27 SEPTEMBER 2018

ARBITRATORS' AUTHORITY: SCOPE AND LIMITATIONS

Horacio A. Grigera Naón

I. External and Internal Factors Fashioning the Scope of Arbitral Authority

The authority of arbitrators has external and internal limitations that have, as a common denominator, the fact that the immediate source of arbitral authority is the will of the parties and not governmental power.

Arbitration is limited by external factors because, unlike national judges, arbitrators are not part of any government and therefore lack imperium to enforce their decisions. Their decisions only become effective to the extent that applicable national laws and courts lend their support to arbitral determinations and awards. In some instances, arbitrators lack the authority to make certain decisions. For example, arbitrators may issue provisional measures in the form of orders addressed to the parties in the dispute. However, unlike national judges, they cannot attach property or otherwise issue orders addressed to non-parties like banks or public registries.

Arbitral power is also limited by internal factors because although party autonomy is the basis, *inter alia*, of arbitral authority to make procedural determinations, weighing the different factors that affect its exercise and limitations is often more art than science. Perhaps the most relevant of internal factors is that, although vested with a certain degree of authority to conduct proceedings and decide administrative matters in the absence of the parties' agreement,[1] when addressing procedural

---

[1] See Article 19, 2012 ICC Arbitration Rules (as amended as of 1 March 2017, ("ICC Rules")) (*"[t]he proceedings before the arbitral tribunal shall be*

matters arbitrators have to persuade (or induce) of their legitimate authority, rather than impose it.

Persuasion, or the ability to induce compliance, is not a given and has to be built up step-by-step from the very inception of the arbitral procedure. The extent to which an arbitral tribunal can induce compliance largely depends on the reasonableness of arbitral procedural determinations and the arbitral tribunal's demeanor during exchanges with the parties. A tribunal will be most successful when its members are courteous and firm and are able to ensure that each party has been properly heard in connection with each procedural determination. The tribunal must show the parties that the arbitrators know and have studied the record, that arbitral decisions will not be made carelessly or irreflexively, and that the parties can rely on the final judgment.

Another element that contributes to the persuasive nature of arbitral procedural determinations, and thus reinforces arbitral authority, is conveying to the parties that the arbitral tribunal operates as a united team when it addresses procedural matters. Showing internal disagreements to the parties and their counsel, rather than addressing these disagreements within the four corners of the internal interactions among the members of the tribunal, undermines arbitral authority and erodes the parties' and their counsels' trust and respect. Of course, this disconnect is more dramatic and harmful when one of the members of the arbitral tribunal openly takes strong positions (for example, through questions during the hearing) favoring the party that appointed him or her. At that point harm is done without reaching the level at which a party would feel comfortable challenging the arbitrator after carefully balancing the resulting disruption of the normal course of the arbitration and the risk of alienating the challenged arbitrator if the accusation failed. That kind of attitude should prompt a private conversation between the president of the arbitral

---

governed by the Rules and, where the Rules are silent, by any rules which the parties or, failing them, the arbitral tribunal may settle on, whether or not reference is thereby made to the rules of procedure of a national law to be applied to the arbitration"), INT'L CHAMBER OF COM., *2012 Arbitration Rules (effective March 1, 2017)*, https://iccwbo.org/dispute-resolution-services/arbitration/rules-of-arbitration/#article_19.

tribunal and the arbitrator, even if that requires pausing the hearing. The president should clearly impress on the arbitrator that he or she must refrain from such conduct that, if not ended, could taint the authority and integrity of the tribunal at large.

There is also a psychological factor that positively contributes to the persuasiveness of arbitral procedural determinations. This includes the parties' and counsels' awareness that the fate of their case is in the hands of the arbitral tribunal and that it would be a mistake to alienate the tribunal by observing improper conduct during procedure with the intention or potential side effect of challenging arbitral authority. Some examples of improper conduct include attempting to delay the procedure through baseless applications; unjustified requests to extend procedural deadlines, requests for the production of documents well after the deadline without a show of good cause; multiplying procedural objections in the hearing; or trying to create procedural land mines for future use to set aside the award.

In this respect, certain external factors (particularly the laws of the seat of the arbitration), combine with the already-described internal ones to enhance arbitral authority and concomitantly deter parties from resorting to improper tactics. Because of the limited means to appeal or set aside arbitral determinations, at least in national jurisdictions that are interested in attracting arbitrations, parties and counsel know that arbitral decisions will finally settle the cases on their merits, leaving very limited chances to attack such determinations before a court of law. For this reason, parties and their counsel may be inclined not to undermine arbitral authority by resorting to procedural tactics that could have a boomerang adverse effect on the outcomes of their cases.

II. Arbitrators' Coercive Powers

In theory, depending on the laws of the jurisdiction of the arbitration, the argument could be made that arbitrators may impose comminatory sanctions, known as *astreintes*, to induce a party to enforce arbitral procedural determinations. However, even if the tribunal had the authority to do so under the applicable law, it would most likely lack the authority to enforce the sanctions, which would be delegated to a national court of law. Be that as it may, I have never been confronted with a situation requiring *astreintes* or situation where a tribunal was asked to impose *astreintes*. I do not believe this to be a common occurrence, as that type of uncooperative conduct would normally pave the way for the arbitral tribunal to draw adverse inferences regarding the case of the recalcitrant party.

Another facet of arbitral authority, in addition to the ability of arbitrators to persuade or induce as referred to in Part I, is using arbitral powers to police the proceedings. Such powers cannot be equated with those of judges in a court of law. Perhaps the most evident power that courts have, and arbitrators lack, is the authority to hold a party or counsel in contempt, to impose fines on counsel, or even to exclude counsel from a proceeding. However, in an exceptional circumstance that arose in a bilateral investment treaty arbitration, the arbitral tribunal decided to exclude counsel from the case where the presence of the excluded counsel could potentially undermine the fairness of the proceedings.[2]

Even if it was accepted that arbitrators have the right to exclude counsel under the applicable law, arbitration rules, or arbitration guidelines, such power would need to be exercised with the utmost care and caution, and only to safeguard the integrity and fairness of the arbitral procedure.[3]

---

[2] *See HEP v. Slovenia (Hrvatska Elektroprivreda v. Republic of Slovenia)*, ICSID Case No. ARB/05/24 (Award) (Dec. 17, 2015), available at: http://icsidfiles.worldbank.org/icsid/ICSIDBLOBS/OnlineAwards/C69/DC7132 _En.pdf. *But see*, *Rompetrol Group N.V. v. Romania*, ICSID Case No. ARB/06/3 (Award) (May 6, 2013). In a later case, the arbitral tribunal took a much more cautious approach regarding the same issue, perhaps partly because the facts were different and did not justify the exclusion of counsel.
[3] *See generally* Int'l B. Ass'n, *Guidelines on Party Representation in International Arbitration* (2013), available at: https://www.ibanet.org/Document/Default.aspx?DocumentUid=6F0C57D7-E7A0-43AF-B76E-714D9FE74D7F; *see also*, INT'L CHAMBER OF COM., *2012 Arbitration Rules (effective March 1, 2017); see also Article 22 (4): Conduct of the Arbitration*, available at: https://iccwbo.org/dispute-resolution-services/arbitration/rules-of-arbitration/#article_22. The guidelines apply if so agreed by the parties or if after consulting with the parties the arbitral tribunal wishes to rely on them "after having determined that it has the authority to rule on matters of Party representation to ensure the integrity and fairness of the

The party's freedom to have and maintain counsel of its own choice is closely associated with due process since it is part and parcel of a party's fundamental right to present and defend its case by hiring a person who enjoys the party's trust because of their personal qualities and professional proficiency. Such right cannot be denied or limited except in extreme circumstances in which the very principle of due process would suffer because maintaining a particular counsel could compromise the integrity of the proceedings and work to the detriment of the opposing party's rights and legitimate expectations.

Another area in which the arbitrators' authority may be tested is within their power to collect evidence. Arbitration rules feature open-ended wording that suggest that arbitrators have such power. However, in practice they are seldom used and should be exercised sparingly.[4] It would be one thing to require the incorporation of the full text of an incomplete document that was already in the record, or of a document that was cross-referenced in another document that was already in the record. It would be a different matter for the arbitral tribunal to *sua sponte* launch evidentiary collection to establish an arbitral record to satisfy its own investigative inclinations. Arbitrators should be ill-advised to involve themselves in such conduct for at least two reasons. First, by so doing they are likely to advantage one party's case to the detriment of the opposing party's case, thus upsetting the apple cart in ways

---

arbitral proceedings." Guidelines 5-6 address, precisely, the *Hrvatska* scenario (*supra* note 2 and corresponding text): "5. Once the Arbitral Tribunal has been constituted, a person should not accept representation of a Party in the arbitration when a relationship exists between the person and an Arbitrator that would create a conflict of interest unless none of the Parties objects after proper disclosure. 6. The Arbitral Tribunal may, in case of breach of Guideline 5, take measures appropriate to safeguard the integrity of the proceedings, including the exclusion of the new Party Representative from participating in all or part of the arbitral proceedings." Int'l B. Ass'n, *Guidelines on Party Representation in International Arbitration* (2013),
https://www.ibanet.org/Document/Default.aspx?DocumentUid=6F0C57D7-E7A0-43AF-B76E-714D9FE74D7F.

[4] *See* INT'L CHAMBER OF COM., *2012 Arbitration Rules (effective March 1, 2017); Article 25 (1): Establishing the Facts of the Case*,
https://iccwbo.org/dispute-resolution-services/arbitration/rules-of-arbitration/#article_25; *see also* Article 22 (5).

contrary to due process and the impartial, independent nature of arbitrators. Second, evidentiary measures are usually costly and time-consuming, and carried out on the parties' time; thus, arbitrators must be very careful not to increase the arbitral procedure costs and duration by taking actions that neither party asked them to take.

III. The Arbitral Tribunal's Internal Chemistry: Dissenting Opinions

Finally, another area in which the authority of the arbitral tribunal may be at issue is when problems arise with the internal chemistry of the members of the arbitral tribunal. This matter has already warranted some attention in Part I of this paper.

Differences of opinion on legal and evidentiary matters among the members of an arbitral tribunal are not unusual when exchanging views on the complex legal and factual questions that usually constitute the subject matter of the disputes at issue. This becomes problematic, however, when disagreements transform into conduct that is designed to derail the arbitration or favor either the setting aside or non-enforcement of the award. Such would be the case, for example, if an arbitrator leaked the substance or direction of deliberations to the party that appointed them, had *ex parte* communications with his or her appointor, or submitted a dissenting opinion to weaken the majority's award, with the intention of exposing it to possible annulment by a court of law on appeal. Such actions have been aptly characterized as "arbitral terrorism."[5]

There are two different views regarding dissenting opinions. The first advocates that dissenting opinions are impermissible because they tend to betray the secrecy of deliberations, undermine the persuasive value and the binding force of arbitral awards, and fail to contribute to the evolution of a non-existent arbitral jurisprudence, as there is no arbitral case law (commercial arbitral awards in principle do not become public) or arbitral *stare decisis*. Further, statistics show that, in almost all cases, dissenting

---

[5] Yves Derains, *The Arbitrator's Deliberation*, 27 AM. U. INT'L L. REV. 911, 918 (2012).

opinions are made by the arbitrator chosen by the losing party. These statistics could be used to argue that arbitrators are invariably partial to the case made by the (losing) party that appointed them.

The second view, which I endorse, takes a more moderate approach. This view asserts that not all dissenting opinions belong in the same category: there are the good and proper dissents, but there are also the bad and ugly. The dissenting opinions that fall into the latter are unprincipled in terms of the consideration of legal arguments put before the arbitrators and the record of the case. Their only purpose or consequence is to weaken the award. The dissenter may also be prompted by the desire to signal to the party that appointed him or her that she or he sided with and staunchly defended the appointing party's views with the expectation of future appointments or as quid pro quo within the context of a preexisting relationship. Such dissents find little to no support in reasoning that is based on the legal and factual questions raised in the dispute.

The good dissents are those with honest conviction that the majority is getting something wrong either on the law, on the facts, or on both. Professional integrity in fulfilling the arbitral function is at the core of the overarching arbitral mission. An arbitrator's integrity—and also his or her reputation—suffer when he or she begins endorsing awards that the arbitrator considers fundamentally wrong on the law or on the facts. In such circumstances, particularly when the law is not applied or is misapplied by the majority, a dissent is justified and even morally required.[6]

Finally, in this, as in many other respects, there may be numerous reasons why statistics are not convincing. As Mark Twain once said: "[t]here are three kinds of lies: lies, damn lies,

---

[6] Despite the absence of precedential value of commercial arbitration awards, the following words of Justice Ruth Bader Ginsburg still ring true for international commercial arbitration: "[t]o sum up, although I appreciate the value of unanimous opinions, I will continue to speak in dissent when important matters are at stake." Ruth Bader Ginsburg, *The Role of Dissenting Opinions*, 95 MINN. L. REV. 1, 7 (2010).

and statistics."[7] In the area of arbitration, particularly regarding dissenting opinions, there is much wisdom in Mark Twain's words. In many instances, statistics are unable to capture the inner workings of the arbitral tribunal that may lead to a dissent: from a weak or inexperienced president who is led by the nose by an astute and partial arbitrator to get to an incorrect or biased decision and thus prompting a dissent by the other arbitrator; to an opinionated president who has a pre- and ill-conceived vision of the case, which is promptly endorsed by one of the arbitrators who immediately sees that the party that appointed him or her will have the upper hand. Either one of these situations, as well as a multitude of others not outlined here, leave the other arbitrator no option but to dissent. These are just examples of possible scenarios justifying a dissenting opinion that are not captured by statistics.

---

[7] Gary Martin, *The Meaning and Origin of the Expression: There are Three Kinds of Lies: Lies, Damned Lies, and Statistics*, The Phrase Finder, https://www.phrases.org.uk/meanings/lies-damned-lies-and-statistics.html. (last visited Nov. 18, 2019).

THE INVESTOR-STATE DISPUTE SETTLEMENT SYSTEM AMIDST CRISIS, COLLAPSE, AND REFORM

Henrique Sachetim [1]* and Rafael Codeço [2]**

ABSTRACT

The dispute settlement regime between investors and states through *ad hoc* arbitration has come under heavy criticism in the past few decades. More recently, these critiques have escalated to the extent that the international community is considering replacing it with a completely new scheme that includes a permanent tribunal to settle such disputes. An intermediate approach to reforming the system—the establishment of an appellate body aimed at providing consistency to the numerous ad hoc arbitration awards—is also being considered. As a third option, the arbitration community, as well as other stakeholders interested in maintaining the *ad hoc* regime, are working to reform it by addressing only some of its flaws, while preserving its fundamental characteristics. This article analyzes the main criticisms of the current dispute settlement regime between investors and states and carries out a comparison between the three policy reform options, how they are intended to solve the system's flaws, as well as the implications arising from each of those options.

---

[1]* Henrique Sachetim is a professor of international law at the Public Law Institute of Brasilia in the disciplines focused on the Law of the World Trade Organization (WTO). He holds a Master in International Law and Economics from the World Trade Institute (Switzerland), a Master in Business Administration from the Federal University of Parana (Brazil) and is currently a Doctorate candidate in Law at the University of São Paulo (Brazil). Henrique also works as a Special Advisor to the Secretary of the Brazilian Foreign Trade Chamber (CAMEX).

[2]** Rafael Codeço is currently a Foreign Trade Analyst at the Ministry of Economy, Brazil. He serves in the Department of International Negotiations of the Foreign Trade Secretariat, taking part in negotiations of international investment agreements and international forums regarding the governance of trade and investment. Rafael has studied Law in his undergraduate studies. He was awarded a MSc. in Globalisation and Development with merit from SOAS, University of London (United Kingdom).

Table of Contents

I. INTRODUCTION	*21*
II. THE INVESTOR-STATE DISPUTE SETTLEMENT CRISIS	*26*
III. THE PROPOSALS TO REFORM THE ISDS	*33*
a. The International Court System	*34*
i. *The ICS and the Shortcomings of the ICS*	*35*
ii. *Trade-offs and Practical Difficulties of the ICS*	*41*
b. Appeals Mechanism	*43*
c. ICSID Reform – The Establishment Strikes Back	*46*
IV. CONCLUSION	*58*

I. Introduction

The current Investor-State Dispute Settlement System (ISDS) was created to allow foreign investors to bring claims directly against the states where the investors placed their investments. It began to provide foreign investors with a set of rules for resolving disputes in cases where the states hosting their investments do not comply with the terms of an international investment agreement (IIA). Its purpose is to protect foreign investors by providing them with an enforceable mechanism in the case of discrimination, expropriation, or any other restrictions of their rights under the IIA. Before the ISDS, disputes about foreign investment were settled either through domestic courts or diplomatic channels, where the investor's state of citizenship would bring a case against the state where the investment was located.[3]

The first proposal for an ISDS, known as the Abs-Shawcross

---

[3] *See* Anthea Roberts, *Power and Persuasion in Investment Treaty Interpretation: The Dual Role of States*, 104 Am. J. Int'l Law 179 (2010).

Draft Convention, emerged during the late 1950s as a formulation from a group of European businesspersons and jurists, without any participation from governments.[4] Among the main arguments in favor of the ISDS was the perception that a reliance on domestic systems would only hold merit in countries with sound legal systems, good governance, and effective local courts.[5] Thus, from the investors' perspective, instead of settling foreign investment disputes before often biased and unsophisticated domestic courts in (developing) host states, most IIAs allowed them to move around the national courts of the host state to international arbitration proceedings.[6]

Moreover, the ISDS safeguards the investors' interests in cases where political considerations in their home countries impede that state from confronting the state hosting the investment.[7] From the point of view of the investor's state, the mechanism prevents disputes concerning individuals from becoming a motive for divergence between sovereign states. From the perspective of the host states, the ISDS avoids possible retaliation from the investor's state, which could materialize even in areas outside the scope of the investment.

This proposal, commonly portrayed as a mechanism to protect foreign investors, proved attractive to capital-exporting countries as it served as inspiration for the dispute settlement mechanism in the IIA, as prescribed by the Organisation for Economic Co-operation and Development (OECD).[8] Ever since, this type of IIA has been presented to developing countries as a vehicle for

---

[4] *See* RUDOLF DOLZER & CHRISTOPH SCHREUER, PRINCIPLES OF INTERNATIONAL INVESTMENT LAW 72 (Oxford Univ.Press 2nd ed. 2012) (ebook).
[5] *See* Reform of Investor-State Dispute Settlement: In Search of a Roadmap, 2 UNCTAD 1, 7 (2013) https://unctad.org/en/PublicationsLibrary/webdiaepcb2013d4_en.pdf.
[6] *See* Joost Pauwelyn, *At the Edge of Chaos?: Foreign Investment Law as a Complex Adaptive System, How It Emerged and How It Can Be Reformed*, 29 ICSID REVIEW 372, 394 (2014).
[7] *Id.*
[8] *See* DOLZER & SCHREUER, *supra* note 4.

attracting foreign investment.

However, after almost six decades of existence, the correlation between Bilateral Investment Treaties (BITs), ISDS clauses and investment attraction is yet to be proven.[9] Yet, the dramatic increase in the number of disputes involving investors and states leaves no room to doubt that the ISDS mechanism has served the alleged purpose of protecting investments.[10] Nonetheless, the ISDS system has garnered numerous criticisms, as shown in the following section, and no longer forms a consensus, even among capital-exporting countries.

The Emergence of a New Paradigm

In the context of the negotiation of the Transatlantic Trade and Investment Partnership (TTIP), the European Union (EU) proposed to address the "fundamental and widespread lack of trust" for the ISDS by introducing an Investment Court System (ICS) to resolve disputes between investors and states.[11] Initially, the ICS was to be

---

[9] An extensive study recently conducted by the Columbia Center on Sustainable Investment (CCSI) concluded that the "evidence that investment treaties have the effect of increasing investment flows is inconclusive" and the "common assumptions about the role of [bilateral investment treaties (BITs)] in attracting foreign investment are unsupported by a considerable amount of quantitative and qualitative evidence". *See* Lise Johnson *et al.*, COSTS AND BENEFITS OF INVESTMENT TREATIES. PRACTICAL CONSIDERATIONS FOR STATES 6 (2018). *See generally* Emma Aisbett, *Bilateral Investment Treaties and Foreign Direct Investment: Correlation versus Causation*, 2255 Munich Personal RePEc Archive (2007); Jason W. Yackee, *Bilateral Investment Treaties, Credible Commitment, and the Rule of (International) Law: Do BITs Promote Foreign Direct Investment?*, 42 LAW & SOC'Y REV 805-832 (2008).; Lauge Poulsen, *The Importance of BITs for Foreign Direct Investment and Political Risk Insurance: Revisiting the Evidence*, Y.B. INT'L INV. LAW & POL'Y 539-574 (2010); Joachim Pohl, *Societal benefits and costs of International Investment Agreements: A critical review of aspects and available empirical evidence*, OECD Working Papers on Int'l Inv. (2018).
[10] *See* KYLA TIENHAARA, *Investor–State dispute settlement*, REGULATORY THEORY: FOUNDATIONS AND APPLICATIONS 676 (Peter Drahos, 2017).
[11] Cecilia Malmstrom, *Proposing an Investment Court System* European Commission (Sept. 16, 2015), https://ec.europa.eu/commission/commissioners/2014-2019/malmstrom/blog/proposing-investment-court-system_en (last visited Mar 16, 2018).

incorporated in bilateral agreements—as is already the case for the Comprehensive Economic and Trade Agreement between the EU and Canada (CETA), and other treaties between the EU and Vietnam, Mexico, and Singapore. Eventually, the courts created under these agreements would be replaced by the Multilateral Investment Court (MIC).

Discussions over ISDS reform are already ongoing in Working Group III (WG III) of the United Nations Commission on International Trade Law (UNCITRAL), whose mandate is separated into three phases, namely to: i) identify concerns regarding the ISDS;[12] (ii) consider whether reform is desirable in light of any identified concerns;[13] and if the Working Group concludes that reform is desirable, (iii) develop any relevant solutions to be recommended to the Commission.[14]

As stated by the secretariat of WG III during its thirty fourth session in November 2017, the options for reform range from a minor adjustment of the existing *ad hoc* system to the creation of

---

[12] In the first phase of its mandate, the WG III concluded that the "concerns commonly expressed about the existing ISDS regime include (i) inconsistency in arbitral decisions, (ii) limited mechanisms to ensure the correctness of arbitral decisions, (iii) lack of predictability, (iv) appointment of arbitrators by parties ("party-appointment"), (v) the impact of party-appointment on the impartiality and independence of arbitrators, (vi) lack of transparency, and (vii) increasing duration and costs of the procedure." *Report of Working Group III (Investor-State Dispute Settlement Reform) on the work of its thirty-sixth session*, UNCITRAL 1, 5, 7, 10, 16 (2018), https://uncitral.un.org/sites/uncitral.un.org/files/draft_report_of_wg_iii_for_the_website.pdf (last visited Jan 16, 2019).

[13] As of the last session of its thirty-sixth session, the WG III concluded that a reform is desirable. From the thirty seventh session on, the WG III will address the relevant solutions to recommend to the commission. Report of Working Group III (Investor-State Dispute Settlement Reform) on the work of its thirty-sixth session, UNCITRAL (2018), https://uncitral.un.org/sites/uncitral.un.org/files/draft_report_of_wg_iii_for_the_website.pdf (last visited Jan 16, 2019). *Id.* at 1, 8.

[14] *See United Nations Commission on International Trade Law Working Group III (Investor-State Dispute Settlement Reform)*, UNCITRAL (2017), 1, 3 https://documents-dds-ny.un.org/doc/UNDOC/LTD/V17/067/48/PDF/V1706748.pdf?OpenElement (last visited Jan 16, 2019).

an appellate body, or even establishing a permanent court to settle disputes regarding international investments.[15]

The Establishment Strikes Back

Concurrently, amid ongoing discussions held by the United Nations Commission on International Trade Law (UNCITRAL), the International Centre for Settlement of Investment Disputes (ICSID)—the world's leading institution devoted to international investment dispute settlement—launched an amendment process and invited its Member States and the general public to suggest topics that merit consideration for reform. Among others, the list of topics for possible amendment envisages modifications that enhance transparency, access to justice, the independence and impartiality of arbitrators, the consistency of awards, and the duration and cost-effectiveness of the proceedings.[16] There are similarities between the list of concerns identified by UNCITRAL WG III and the topics for possible amendment from the ICSID, showing that reform is symptomatic and that the ICSID wants to address those concerns and improve its functioning before the crisis intensifies and more damages come to the fore.

Three possible outcomes could arise from the abovementioned ISDS reform initiatives. The success of the ongoing WG III process could result in the creation of a permanent court, which would be a radical departure from the current *ad hoc* system. Extensive support for this prospective court would deliver a significant blow to the existing ISDS mechanism.[17] In turn, the creation of an appellate mechanism responsible for reviewing the awards of *ad hoc* tribunals would represent an intermediate solution, where the *ad hoc* tribunals would maintain part of their adjudicatory authority, while transferring the other part to an appellate body. In the third scenario, an ICSID amendment process

---

[15] *See Possible reform of Investor-State dispute settlement (ISDS)*, United Nations Commission on International Trade Law Working Group III (Investor-State Dispute Settlement Reform), UNCITRAL 1, 10-11 (2017), https://undocs.org/A/CN.9/WG.III/WP.142.

[16] *See infra* note 53. The complete list of areas for possible amendment is described in greater detail.

[17] The terms permanent court and International Court System (ICS) are used interchangeably in this paper.

would merely reform the *ad hoc* system, while maintaining its main characteristics.

Each of these reform options presents different solutions to the current ISDS crisis. Consequently, each of them has its advantages and drawbacks. These three reform options affect the interests of stakeholders in different ways, namely investors, states, and the arbitration community. With the aim to assess the adequacy of the reform options in light of identified concerns, the next section of this paper will proceed with an analysis of the most commonly identified flaws of the ISDS. After that, it shifts to assessing the reform options and their likely outcomes, how they would affect ISDS proceedings, and how they would address the system's current challenges.

II.   The Investor-State Dispute Settlement Crisis

While many of its benefits are still valid, the ISDS mechanism has presented several flaws that have raised questions about the system. Thus, many initiatives have emerged that aim to cope with some of the problems pointed out by commentators and practitioners of international investment law. Despite several changes to the IIAs and the arbitration institutions throughout the years, central flaws still remain.[18] Some of these weaknesses cast doubt on the system's ability to attract investment or its capacity to benefit both investors and host countries in a sustainable way. Consequently, this section addresses the specific criticisms of the system's capacity to conduct impartial and efficient procedures for the settlement of investment-related disputes.

Same Facts, Similar Treaty Provisions — Different Outcomes

One of the main criticisms of ISDS proceedings is the inconsistency of arbitral decisions. The cases are judged by a variety of *ad hoc* tribunals, which is widely considered the characteristic that most impedes the consistency and interpretive continuity of case law. Therefore, *ad hoc* tribunals are intrinsically inadequate to ensure the consistency of a system of standards or the development of coherent case law. This is because its mission

---

[18] *See* Pauwelyn, *supra* note 6, at 408.

is to resolve specific cases in a manner that the parties concerned find satisfactory, irrespective of any contradictions within the consolidated understanding or the consequences it could have on future disputes.[19]

Moreover, some legal standards, due to their level of abstraction, allow for different interpretations between arbitral courts. The lack of clarity of the provisions contained in investment agreements and the exponential increase in IIAs containing ISDS provisions have raised the risk of conflicting awards in parallel proceedings. This is because an investor established in multiple countries can claim breaches of the same IIA clause in any of their established countries and the state hosting their investment. Thus, investors can seek relief through multiple *ad hoc* tribunals for the same breach in a single investment, hoping that at least one tribunal will issue an award favorable to their interests.[20]

Under this dynamic, a single dispute can lead to the undesirable situation for the international investment regime in which the same facts and the same treaty provision give rise to inconsistent arbitral decisions in different *ad hoc* tribunals.[21] As a result, the inconsistency of decisions creates uncertainties about the meaning of key investment treaty provisions, leading to a lack of predictability as to how these provisions will be interpreted in the future.

Many Flaws, Little Accountability

Additionally, there are limited mechanisms to ensure the correctness of arbitral decisions, which prevent the system from overturning inconsistencies. ISDS awards are subject to revision or annulment in very limited cases under the ICSID Convention.[22]

---

[19] *See* Mark Feldman, *Investment Arbitration Appellate Mechanism Options: Consistency, Accuracy, and Balance of Power*, 32 ICSID REVIEW 1, 9, N.28 (2017).
[20] *See* Roberts, *supra* note 3.
[21] *See* UNCTAD, *supra* note 5, at 3.
[22] *Post-Award Remedies - ICSID Convention Arbitration*, ICSID, https://icsid.worldbank.org/en/Pages/process/Post-Award-Remedies-Convention-Arbitration.aspx (last visited Nov. 3, 2019).

The only circumstance under which a revision can be required, as stated by Arbitration Rule (AR) 51(1) of the ICSID Convention, is the "discovery of some fact of such a nature as decisively to affect the award, provided that when the award was rendered that fact was unknown to the Tribunal and to the applicant and that the applicant's ignorance of that fact was not due to negligence."[23]

As for requests for annulment, AR 52(1) of the ICSID convention enumerates five circumstances for its application: a) improper constitution of the tribunal, b) excess of power, c) corruption, d) departure from a fundamental rule of procedure, and e) failure to state the reasons on which the award is based. Therefore, under the ICSID Convention, there is no possibility to annul or correct an award, even after having identified manifest errors of law. Furthermore, given that annulment committees are created on an *ad hoc* basis for the purpose of a single dispute, these may also arrive at inconsistent conclusions.[24]

Party Appointment, Impartiality and Independence

The party-appointment system is another issue that often receives criticism for being inherently contradictory to the obligation of arbitrators to be independent and impartial. The insufficiency of these standards under the ICSID has been identified as the cause of the numerous challenges placed against arbitrators in recent disputes,[25] suggesting that disputing parties often perceive a bias or predisposition among arbitrators toward a specific outcome.[26] The fact that parties do not appear to only choose arbitrators based on their experience and skills, but also based on whether the arbitrator enhances their chances of winning a case has given rise to a category of conflicts of interest known as "issue conflicts."[27] This refers to arbitrators who have repeatedly

---

[23] *See* ICSID, supra note 22.
[24] *See* UNCTAD, *supra* note 5, at 3-4.
[25] *See* Maria Nicole Cleis, *The Independence and Impartiality of ICSID Arbitrators*, ANALYSIS OF EXISTING REFORM PROPOSALS 188 (2017) (eBook).
[26] *See* UNCTAD, *supra* note 5, at 4.
[27] *See* Cleis, *supra* note 24, at 191; *see also* David Gaukrodger & Kathryn Gordon, *Investor-State Dispute Settlement: A Scoping Paper for the Investment Policy Community*, OECD Working Papers on International Investment 24

acted as arbitrators or counsels in cases that raised similar issues, allowing the parties in the dispute to identify an arbitrator's propensity to decide a case according to their interests.

One of the characteristics of the ISDS that promotes this "issue conflict" is the fact that most cases are judged by a small group of individuals, making it much easier for the parties to identify the arbitrators' positions. According to a study conducted between 1972 and 2014, 419 different arbitrators sat on ICSID tribunals throughout that time.[28] Although more than half of these arbitrators were appointed for only one case, 10 percent of them accounted for half of the appointments.[29] Similar research found that 247 of the 450 known ISDS disputes occurring in 2012 (not limited to ICSID) were decided by only 15 arbitrators.[30]

Identifying the propensity of an arbitrator toward certain decisions is made easier by the fact that disputes over international investment agreements repeatedly address a limited and uniform number of legal provisions.[31] In addition to the small group of professionals that act as arbitrators and the reduced number of uniform substantive rules discussed before arbitral tribunals, the fact that earlier arbitration decisions are often used as interpretive norms in subsequent cases further allows parties to foresee arbitrators' arguments for future cases.[32] Therefore, by surveying awards issued by arbitrators in past cases, the parties in the dispute can foresee the position arbitrators are likely to adopt in a future case.

As for the arbitrators, their impartiality is commonly questioned for having incentives to favor either investors or states

---

(2012).
[28] Sergio Puig, *Social Capital in the Arbitration Market*, 25 The European Journal of International Law 387, 403 (2014).
[29] *Id.*
[30] Pia Pia Eberhardt & Cecilia Olivet, *Profiting from injustice. How law firms, arbitrators and financiers are fueling an investment arbitration boom*, CORPORATE EUROPE OBSERVATORY AND THE TRANSNATIONAL INSTITUTE 38 (Helen Burley, 2012) (eBook).
[31] UNCTAD, Investor-State Dispute Settlement: A sequel, UNCTAD 96 (2014) (eBook).
[32] *See* Roberts, *supra* note 3.

in their decisions to ensure reappointment in future cases.[33] They are also questioned for an act that could potentially constitute a conflict of interest, known as "double-hatting." This is where an arbitrator also acts as an academic or a legal counsel in a different case. Indeed, their previous position when acting as a counsel, or their argument made in an academic paper, for example, could be a sign of a position they would be likely to defend in a future case.

Opaque Proceedings, Low Legitimacy (Lack of Transparency)

The lack of transparency of ISDS proceedings, with justice being administered "behind closed doors," remains an important criticism levied against the current ISDS regime.[34] Even though this issue has been the focus of some recent reforms, ISDS adjudicatory proceedings can still be kept fully confidential, even in cases that encompass issues of public interest.[35] In order to allow for more transparent proceedings, commentators often suggest measures such as granting public access to arbitration documents and arbitral hearings, as well as allowing the participation of interested third-parties, such as civil society organizations.[36] Such improvements would allow for public participation in the proceedings, which could enhance public understanding of the process and provide all ISDS parties with a greater understanding of the way arbitral tribunals interpret investment protection standards.

Moreover, the lack of transparency, coupled with the accelerated development of international investment law jurisprudence, is considered a factor that prevent states from participating in ISDS disputes on an equal footing. The exponential proliferation of awards and the diffuse nature of the *ad hoc* system, which lacks an organized structure to classify decisions and identify the most important awards for jurisprudence purposes, make it difficult for states to stay up to date with relevant

---

[33] *See* Cleis, *supra* note 24, at 191-92.
[34] *See* UNCITRAL, *supra* note 14, at 12.
[35] *See* UNCTAD, *supra* note 5, at 3.
[36] Rob Howse, *Designing a Multilateral Investment Court: Issues and Options*, 36 Y.B. EUR. LAW 209, 235 (2017).

developments in ISDS jurisprudence. This task requires time and expertise. Very often, it is not achieved, because of the states' limited bureaucratic resources and budget constraints.[37]

Long Proceedings, High Costs, and Expensive Awards

As emphasized in the previous paragraph, ISDS arbitration is getting progressively more complex and expensive, which in turn imposes serious barriers to the access to justice. Host countries have faced long-lasting cases with high-value claims and awards that were not expected when the system was created, casting doubt on the idea that arbitration is synonymous with a speedy and low-cost method of dispute resolution.[38] [39]

Complexity of the cases and the open-ended nature of many of the legal issues in dispute lead to high costs and extended lengths of proceedings. Ultimately, this leads to the need to study numerous previous arbitral awards and other legal sources. Due to its complexity, investment arbitration is dominated by big law firms that mobilize large teams of lawyers, employ sophisticated techniques, and charge high fees for their services, further undermining access to the mechanism.[40]

In fact, case law shows that filing and winning an investment claim takes time and requires a considerable amount of money. The average duration of an ICSID arbitration procedure typically takes three to four years.[41] On average, the costs for each party in a single dispute surpasses $8 million,[42] but can exceed $30 million in some cases.[43] Australia, for example, is reported to have spent nearly $40 million on a recent dispute against a cigarette

---

[37] *See* Roberts, *supra* note 3.
[38] *See* UNCTAD, *supra* note 5, at 4.
[39] *Id.*
[40] *Id.*
[41] *See Proposals for Amendment of the ICSID Rules*, ICSID 898 (Aug. 2, 2018) (unpublished manuscript) (on file with ICSID).
[42] *See* David Gaukrodger & Kathryn Gordon, *Investor-State Dispute Settlement: A Scoping Paper for the Investment Policy Community*, OECD Working Papers on International Investment 24 (2012).
[43] *See* Gaukrodger & Gordon, *supra* note 41, at 19.

company.[44]

Arbitrators' fees alone cost, on average, $700,000,[45] which is estimated to represent just 16 percent of the total cost of arbitration proceedings.[46] Legal counsel represents the largest cost component to the parties which are estimated to represent, on average, 82 percent of the total arbitration cost. Meanwhile, institutional costs payable to organizations that administer the arbitration process amount to about 2 percent of the total.[47]

Therefore, it is understandable that certain respondent States may struggle to come up with the significant resources required to properly defend themselves in the current ISDS system.[48] At the same time, the average cost for arbitration in the ICSID and the average time for the conclusion of a case are also a concern for investors with limited resources, especially small and medium ones.[49] In that sense, the ISDS mechanism, despite allowing foreign investors to have direct access to international arbitration, could be considered an ineffective regime that only protects the wealthiest investors, since only a few could be able to take advantage of it.[50]

Other elements that exacerbate the mechanism's flaws are the high-value claims and expensive awards verified in arbitral proceedings. Many ISDS claims now exceed $1 billion,[51] and have reached $114 billion,[52] which would present a challenge to the public finances of any country, let alone developing ones.[53]

---

[44] *See id.*
[45] *See* Pauwelyn, *supra* note 6, at 394.
[46] *See* Gaukrodger & Gordon, *supra* note 41, at 19.
[47] *See id.*
[48] *See* Howse, *supra* note 35, at 231.
[49] *See* Pauwelyn, *supra* note 6, at 380.
[50] *See id.*
[51] *See* TIENHAARA, *supra* note 10, at 683.
[52] *See* UNCTAD, *supra* note 5, at 3.
[53] *See* TIENHAARA, *supra* note 10, at 686.

III.   The Proposals to Reform the ISDS

Notwithstanding the long-standing criticism over the *ad hoc* ISDS the best way to address the current crisis remains unclear. There are three main courses of action being considered. One is the creation of an ICS, which is the most radical departure from the current system and is being voiced by the EU and its allies. It envisages the comprehensive replacement of the current system with a two-tier permanent court made up of functionally independent judges with fixed terms. An intermediate approach is the simple establishment of an appellate body aimed at enhancing the consistency of the decisions issued by the arbitral tribunals, while maintaining the core principles of the *ad hoc* system. Finally, the third course of action would be the adoption of incremental modifications to the current system in order to address the main concerns that have been voiced against it, all while maintaining its main characteristics.[54]

---

[54] The division proposed in this article is envisaged to better assess the current initiatives to reform the ISDS. It differs significantly from the authors who analyze the issue under the criteria of depth of the reform, for whom the reform of the ISDS is divided in three main camps: "1. *Incrementalists* view the criticisms of the current system as overblown and argue that Investor-State arbitration remains the best option available. Hence, they favor retaining the existing dispute resolution system but instituting modest reforms that would redress specific concerns. 2. *Systemic reformers* see merit in retaining investors' ability to file claims directly on the international level, but view Investor-State arbitration as a seriously flawed system for dealing with such claims. They champion more significant, systemic reforms, such as replacing Investor-State arbitration with a MIC and appellate body. 3. *Paradigm shifters* dismiss the existing system as irrevocably flawed and in need of wholesale replacement. They reject the utility of investors' making international claims against states, whether before arbitral tribunals or international courts. They embrace a variety of alternatives, such as domestic courts, ombudsmen, and State-to-State arbitration." Anthea Roberts, *Incremental, Systemic, and Paradigmatic Reform of Investor-State Arbitration*, 112 Am. J. Int'l Law 1 (2018). *See also* Sergio Puig & Gregory Shaffer, *Imperfect Alternatives: Institutional Choice and the Reform of Investment Law*, 112 AM. J. INT'L LAW 361, (2018). at 363. They classify the changes under the criteria of institutional alternatives for resolving investment disputes, such as negotiation and mediation; domestic dispute settlement mechanisms such as courts, specialized processes and ombudsman offices; independent interstate adjudicatory mechanisms such as *ad hoc* tribunals and international courts; and international adjudicatory mechanisms as

a. The International Court System

The EU has championed the idea of a permanent court. The majority of EU countries have traditionally been enthusiastic participants of the system. In 2014, however, while reacting to a public consultation[55] on investment protection amid growing concerns over the ISDS in the context of the TTIP negotiations, the Europeans came to advocate for a permanent court to settle disputes between investors and states, first for the TTIP and later for other trade agreements.[56] Even though the TTIP negotiations ended in 2017, the EU managed to implement a permanent investment court in its bilateral agreements with Canada,[57] Vietnam (EU-Vietnam FTA),[58] Singapore (EU-Singapore FTA),[59] and Mexico (EU-Mexico FTA).[60] In 2017, UNCITRAL entrusted its WG III with a mandate to work on a possible reform of the ISDS. One of the reform options being considered by WG III is the creation of a permanent court, whose arbitrators would be tasked with resolving ISDS cases that fall under its jurisdiction.[61] WG III has identified several concerns with the current ISDS system. In the next section, we analyze how a permanent court would be likely to address those concerns.

---

complementary, which include the international review of domestic decisions, international claims after domestic proceedings and interpretation at the request of national courts.

[55] *See Online public consultation on investment protection and investor-to-state dispute settlement (ISDS) in the Transatlantic Trade and Investment Partnership Agreement (TTIP)*, European Commission 25 (Jan. 13, 2015) (on file with European Commission).

[56] *The Multilateral Investment Court project*, European Commission (Dec. 21, 2016), http://trade.ec.europa.eu/doclib/press/index.cfm?id=1608 (last visited Jan 23, 2019).

[57] Comprehensive Economic and Trade Agreement, Can.-EU, Oct. 30, 2016.

[58] EU-Vietnam Investment Protection Agreement, EU-Viet, 2018.

[59] Free Trade Agreement between the European Union and the Republic of Singapore, EU-Sing, Oct. 19, 218.

[60] EU-Mexico Trade Agreement, EU-Mex., Apr. 21, 2018.

[61] *See* UNCITRAL, *supra* note 15.

i. *The ICS and the Shortcomings of the ISDS*

Ensuring the Consistency and Predictability of Tribunal Awards

Champions of the ICS argue that a permanent court would address the ISDS concerns in many ways. As for the lack of consistency, predictability, and certainty of tribunal awards, its advocates state that a consistent jurisprudence can only arise when the parties are obligated to use the same court for the settlement of various disputes. A permanent tribunal would thus ensure the performance of a fixed group of judges for a certain period of time, as well as the opportunity for interaction on a repeated basis, which could potentially reinforce the consistency and coherence of awards.[62]

A standing body of jurists—who repeatedly examine a large number of cases and capture the evolution of the doctrine—would likely be in a privileged position to construct a stable jurisprudence based on precedent case law, thus enhancing the predictability of the system as a whole.[63] Moreover, two key characteristics of permanent courts—the exclusive dedication and repeated interactions of its members—provide for a higher level of engagement and a greater responsibility as an institution, which tends to circumscribe their actuation under the constitutive instruments of the body,[64] thus preventing undesirable outcomes, such as the emergence of inconsistent case law. Besides that, a permanent court, by accumulating the competence over a high number of cases, can enact provisions that consolidate parallel proceedings to avoid different outcomes arising from similar facts.[65]

---

[62] *See* Feldman, *supra* note 19, at 9.
[63] *See* Howse, *supra* note 35, at 226.
[64] *See* Feldman, *supra* note 19.
[65] *See* Article 8.43 - Consolidation (CETA), Lewik, https://www.lewik.org/term/11197/article-843-consolidation-ceta/ (Last visited Nov. 3, 2019) "When two or more claims that have been submitted separately pursuant to Article 8.23 have a question of law or fact in common and arise out of the same events or circumstances, a disputing party or the disputing parties, jointly, may seek the establishment of a separate division of the Tribunal pursuant to this Article and request that such division issue a consolidation order

The abovementioned improvement carries an important side effect with it: the more consistent and predictable the system is, the more prepared the states will be to self-regulate in a way that avoids future disputes. Consequently, there would be a reduction in the so-called "chilling effect"[66] on new regulations that pursue public policy objectives, given that members would be more aware of their regulatory boundaries than they are today. The final result would be more investment and better-designed public policy measures.

More Mechanisms to Pursue the Correctness of Awards

Apart from enhancing consistency, the ICS proposal also aims to provide additional alternatives to ensure the correctness of arbitral awards. As emphasized in the previous section, the ICSID Arbitration Rules provide very few possibilities for the revision and annulment of arbitral awards, possible only on the grounds of serious events.[67] Proponents of the ICS advocate for more alternatives to revise awards in the event of procedural or substantial errors of law, including the re-examination of the case

---

("request for consolidation")." *See also supra* note 57, at 75. Article 3.59.1: "In case that two or more claims submitted under this Section have a question of law or fact in common and arise out of the same events and circumstances, the respondent may submit to the President of the Tribunal a request for the consolidation of such claims or part thereof."

[66] *See* Howse, *supra* note 35, at 235 "... which invites regulatory chill, leading to uncertainty
about the policy space available for States to pursue legitimate regulatory objectives
in the public interest.".

[67] *See* ICSID Convention, *supra* note 22. The only circumstance under which a revision can be required, as stated by the Arbitration Rule 51 of the ICSID convention: [a] party can apply for revision of the award if it discovers a new fact that could decisively affect that award (Article 51 of the ICSID Convention, Arbitration Rules 50, 51, 53 and 54). The new fact must have been unknown to the Tribunal and the applicant when the award was rendered, and the applicant's ignorance of the fact cannot be due to negligence." As for requests of annulment, Arbitration Rule 52 enumerates five circumstances: a) improper constitution of the tribunal, b) excess of power, c) corruption, d) departure from a fundamental rule of procedure and e) failure to state the reasons on which the award is based.

by conducting a comprehensive and fresh analysis of the facts or a limited analysis through checking manifest errors in the appreciation of facts.[68] Therefore, it seems clear that the ICS proposal, encompassing a double-tiered tribunal with an appellate body entrusted with the responsibility of reviewing first-instance awards, would provide a greater possibility of ensuring the integrity of the decisions.

Party Appointment Affecting Arbitrators' Independence and Impartiality

A permanent tribunal is also likely to address the concerns over the lack of independence and impartiality resulting from the party appointment of arbitrators on ISDS *ad hoc* tribunals. Establishing an objective criterion to appoint judges to cases, which would replace the party-appointment system, is already an important step towards adjudicative impartiality.[69] Adjudicators that do not rely on parties to appoint them to a case will naturally enjoy more autonomy to decide the cases, independently of parties' interests.

Besides that, by maintaining a permanent body of adjudicators that is also financially independent from investors' influence, the ICS would be in a better position to implement an ambitious code of conduct that prohibits arbitrators from acting as a counsel in pending or new investment disputes, as well as from being assigned to cases that would create direct or indirect conflicts of interest.[70] Indeed, it is difficult to envisage such a strict code of

---

[68] *See Commission staff working document impact assessment. Multilateral reform of investment dispute resolution,* European Union 11 (2017), https://eur-lex.europa.eu/legal-content/EN/TXT/?uri=CELEX:52017SC0302 (last visited Jan 23, 2019).
[69] *See supra* note 25, 2011-21; *see also* Howse, *supra* note at 235.
[70] Some provisions in this regard are already in place in some agreements negotiated by the EU. See
Article 8.30.1 - Consolidation (CETA), Lewik,
https://www.lewik.org/term/11183/article-830-ethics-ceta/ (Last visited Nov. 3, 2019), which prohibits adjudicators from acting as counsel or as a party-appointed expert or witness in any pending or new investment dispute under CETA or any other international agreement—a rule that does not exist in the ICSID convention. The same article also impedes members of the tribunal from being affiliated with any government, from taking instructions from any organization or government with regard to matters related to the dispute, and

conduct in the current ISDS, where arbitrators have no assurance of future income and are thus compelled to find other sources of income. Since those individuals have considerable knowledge about international investment dispute resolution, they naturally tend to use their expertise by acting in other positions in ISDS cases.

Transparency

Given that "the concern over lack of transparency or justice being administered behind closed doors remains an important criticism levied against the current ISDS regime,"[71] it is expected that the prospective ICS is likely to address the issue of transparency. Demands for greater transparency in investment dispute proceedings include the possibility of non-party intervention (*amicus curiae* briefs), disclosure of documents and information from the proceedings, as well as publicly accessible hearings.[72]

One indication that the procedural rules of the prospective ICS would focus heavily on the issue of transparency comes from the permanent investment courts established in the new agreements that the EU recently negotiated with Canada, Vietnam, Singapore, and Mexico. By incorporating the UNCITRAL Transparency Rules—with some modifications—these agreements require that the hearings, written submissions, tribunal awards, and the relevant documents of the dispute be open to the public, unless there is a need to protect confidential and sensible information. Moreover, the transparency provisions of those agreements allow for *amicus curiae* briefs, stipulating the circumstances under which non-disputing parties can participate in the proceedings.[73]

Apart from granting a greater level of transparency, the

---

from participating in the consideration of any disputes that would create a direct or indirect conflict of interest. *See also* Article 3.40.1 *supra* note 57 at 53.
[71] UNCITRAL 2017, *supra* note 15, at 7.
[72] *See* Howse, *supra* note 35, at 235.
[73] Transparency provisions are placed on the article 8.36 of the CETA; article 46 of the Dispute Settlement Chapter of EU-Vietnam FTA, and article 19 of EU-Mexico FTA, and annex 8 of the EU-Singapore FTA.

incorporation of those rules by permitting the oversight of the proceedings, would allow for a greater understanding of the adjudicators' judgments. It could represent a paradigmatic shift from a system where case law evolves without proper awareness to one where the relevant stakeholders would be able to better assess the prevailing understandings and doctrines regarding the language of IIAs, thus improving the consistency and predictability of the system.

Reducing the Costs and Duration of Proceedings: The Issue of Access to Justice

The high costs and excessive duration of the proceedings are emphasized by UNCITRAL WG III as the main concerns of the ISDS and are addressed in the ICS. ISDS costs are constructed of fees paid to arbitrators, administrative fees charged by arbitral institutions and fees paid by the parties to their counsels for legal representation and for experts.[74] As highlighted in the previous section, the lion's share of ISDS costs are spent on legal counsel,[75] whereas costs for arbitrators and tribunal fees constitute only a small portion of it.[76] Thus, ISDS tribunal proceedings entail very low overhead costs.[77] A permanent court, on the other hand, would require permanent funding to cover the salary of its permanent body of adjudicators, as well as the maintenance of the tribunal's structure.

This rationale could lead to the conclusion that an ICS would increase ISDS costs. However, it is reasonable to assume that the standardization of adjudication procedures would bring efficiency to dispute resolution and make it less time-consuming. This would

---

[74] *See supra* note 14, at 9-10.
[75] *See* Gaukrodger & Gordon, *supra* note 41, at 15.
[76] *See* Matthew Hodgson & Alastair Campbell, *Damages and costs in investment treaty arbitration revisited*, THE INT'L J. COM. TREATY ARB. (2017), https://globalarbitrationreview.com/article/1151755/damages-and-costs-in-investment-treaty-arbitration-revisited (last visited Jan 23, 2019). The authors conclude that the sum of costs paid to legal counsel and experts ($10.9 million) is approximately 9.85 times greater than the average tribunal cost ($1.1 million).
[77] *See* Joerg Risse, *A new "investment court system" Reasonable Proposal or Nonstarter?,* Global Arbitration News (Sept. 25, 2015), https://globalarbitrationnews.com/investment-court-system-20150925.

presumably lead to a reduction in the hours worked by experts and legal counsel, thus decreasing the overall money spent on the largest cost component of the ISDS.[78] A more consistent jurisprudence can reduce discrepancies among the value of awards, bringing more certainty to how much parties are expected to spend to bring a case before an investment tribunal.

Furthermore, an ICS, by concentrating numerous disputes in the same adjudicative body, would increase the economies of scale by consolidating the various claims that have arisen from the same circumstance. Take, as an example, Argentina's response to its financial crises, which generated several disputes with investors from different countries, even though the background and the causes of the claims were the same.[79] In such a case, *ad hoc* tribunals are likely to spend time and energy on each individual claim under a different tribunal, whereas an ICS could consolidate those claims, thus sparing important resources.

Moreover, the ICS would also permit the elaboration of a scheme envisaged to reduce the burden that some users currently face in filing a claim for international investment arbitration. While a permanent court would require permanent funding to cover overhead costs, these could be favorably allocated to certain categories of economically disadvantaged users—taking into consideration their capacity to cover the tribunal's costs. Under such mechanism, both developing countries and small and medium enterprises would benefit.

A more predictable system also tends to reduce the parties' expenses on legal counsel and experts. The lack of a rule of binding precedent may place a burden on parties and their legal counsels to submit all available arguments, irrespective of whether those arguments have been accepted or rejected by earlier tribunals.[80] The fact that many legal issues remain unsettled

---

[78] *See* Robert W. Schwieder, *TTIP and the Investment Court System: A New (and Improved?) Paradigm for Investor-State Adjudication*, COLUMB. J. TRANSNAT'L L., 178, 199 (2016).
[79] *See* Howse, *supra* note 35.
[80] *See* Report of Working Group III (Investor-State Dispute Settlement Reform)

imposes the necessity on legal counsel and experts to invest extensive resources into studying numerous previous arbitral wards in order to develop a legal position.[81] Ultimately, all these costs are borne by the parties of the ISDS disputes.

ICS and the Balance of Power

In addition to the points debated above, an ICS would be in a better position to fix the opposing forces that currently threaten the equilibrium of disputes between investors and states. The vague wording of existing IIAs[82] allow adjudicators to make overly broad interpretations, while the *ad hoc* nature of the ISDS system allows the parties to choose arbitrators who are more susceptible to deciding the case according to their interests.[83] This combination exacerbates the risk of an asymmetrical power balance between investors and states. This risk is especially high in disputes involving billionaire multinational companies that are able to devote considerable financial resources to elite arbitrators/counsel who are anchored in commercial law firms.[84] Moreover, the lack of mechanisms to oversee such risks enhances the widespread sentiment of distrust in the ISDS.[85] Therefore, the settlement of disputes in a more institutionalized regime would provide greater levels of independence and create control mechanisms that, in turn, would reduce the risks of adjudicators exceeding their mandates.

ii.   *Trade-offs and Practical Difficulties of the ICS*

The shift from the *ad hoc* ISDS to an ICS implies certain costs and drawbacks that do not exist under the current system. A permanent court would result in overhead costs to maintain its physical facilities, along with the necessity to pay the salaries of a

---

on the work of its thirty-fourth session, *supra* note 72, at 8.
[81] *See* UNCTAD, *supra* note 5.
[82] Charles H. Brower II, *Investor-State Disputes under NAFTA: The Empire Strikes Back*, 43 COLUMB. J. TRANSNAT'L L. 56 (2001), https://digitalcommons.wayne.edu/lawfrp/165 (last visited Jan 23, 2019). He argues that the inclusion of intentionally vague terms in IIAs are "designed to give adjudicators a quasi-legislative authority to articulate a variety of rules necessary to achieve the treaty's object and purpose in particular disputes."
[83] *See* Schweider, *supra* note 76.
[84] *See* Howse, *supra* note 35.
[85] *See* TIENHAARA, *supra* note 10.

standing body of judges—costs that do not currently exist. Another negative aspect of an ICS would be the lack of finality that could result from the adoption of an appellate mechanism. Advocates of this argument opine that the great merits of arbitration—its speed and finality—would eventually be undermined in an appeals system that would likely be frequently invoked.[86] While this criticism merits consideration, it is worth recalling that an appellate body has the function of ensuring the correctness of award decisions and enhancing the legitimacy of the system. Moreover, the extra costs and delays that may arise from an ICS can be compensated and even surpassed by the gains of scale and efficiency achieved through a greater standardization of procedures, as addressed in the previous section.

The ICS also faces criticism over the practical difficulties of its implementation. First, the highly diverse universe of more than 3,000 international investment agreements, each with their different wordings and negotiation histories, would add a high degree of complexity to the operation of the court, especially in the development of consistent jurisprudence.[87] Other issues include the lack of specialized personnel that would form the pool of arbitrators of the ICS, its ability to select high-quality judges,[88] and whether they would really be any different from the experts who regularly intervene in Investor-State arbitrations.[89] Furthermore, as

---

[86] *See* Michael Wood, *Choosing between Arbitration and a Permanent Court: Lessons from Inter-State Cases*, 32 ICSID REVIEW 1-16 (2017). *See also* Feldman, *supra* note 19.

[87] *See* Howse, *supra* note 35.

[88] *See* Wood, *supra* note 84.

[89] Nikos Lavranos, *The Shortcomings of the Proposal for an "International Court System" (ICS)* EFILA Blog (2016), https://efilablog.org/2016/02/02/the-shortcomings-of-the-proposal-for-an-international-court-system-ics/ (last visited Jan 23, 2019). "Apart from this danger, it remains doubtful whether a sufficient number of appropriately qualified individuals with the necessary expertise can be found. This is particularly true since many professionals currently working in arbitration may be excluded on the basis that they could be considered to be biased. The pool of TFI and AT judges would seem to be limited to academics, (former) judges and (former) Governmental officials. That might not be sufficient to guarantee the practical experience and expertise needed and/or independence from the State."

is frequently invoked by the arbitration industry, the party-appointment system has the effect of enhancing investor trust in the ISDS. Therefore, in such a system where only the states would be able to establish arbitrators, the investors' trust in the system could be undermined.[90]

Although this shift would certainly bring several collateral effects, as is the case for any paradigm shift, its consequences should not be appraised individually, since they could be compensated by other advantages. Indeed, case studies show that most ISDS cases deal with only a few disciplines, with similar wordings, contradicting the affirmation that the more than 3,000 IIAs would make it difficult for an ICS to develop consistent jurisprudence.

Even though it may be true that there might be a shortage of individuals in the pool of arbitrators in the first years after the implementation of an ICS, its implementation is likely to generate, throughout the years, the specialized personnel required for its proper functioning. As for the overhead costs that would be created by an ICS, it is reasonable to assume that the gains of scale caused by the consolidation of multiple cases under a single tribunal would equal or even surpass this burden. Likewise, investor distrust arising from the elimination of party appointment would be compensated through improving the consistency and the predictability of the system as a whole.

b. Appeals Mechanism

The creation of an appeals mechanism would represent an intermediate reform of the international investment dispute resolution mechanism by creating a standing body of jurists with the competence to review decisions of the arbitral tribunals, while maintaining the functioning dynamics of the *ad hoc* system—in keeping with the interests of the arbitration industry. This reform option is envisaged to address some of the most common concerns over the ISDS, which were already addressed in the previous

---

[90] *Id.* "The pre-selection of the TFI and AT judges by the Contracting Parties carries the inherent risk of selecting 'pro-State' individuals, in particular since they are paid by the States (or rather their tax payers) alone."

sections. These include the lack of mechanisms to ensure the correctness of tribunal awards, as well as a lack of consistency and predictability in the system. On the other hand, it does not tackle other issues, such as the impact of party appointment on the impartiality and independence of arbitrators and the lack of transparency.

The idea of the creation of an appellate body in the ICSID emerged within the last decade. Similar schemes were effectively negotiated in some regional agreements—mainly by the United States with the Dominican Republic and Central America (CAFTA-DR), Singapore, Peru, Morocco, Korea, and Chile.[91] Apart from the examples coming from the US, India's newest generation of BITs also indicates an openness to a future appellate mechanism.[92]

In 2004, the ICSID discussed the implementation of an appeals mechanism in a discussion paper on possible improvements to the investment arbitration framework.[93] More recently, this option resurged in discussions on the reform of the international investment regime as a means to achieve greater consistency, coherence, and predictability in investment arbitration case law,[94] and it is frequently suggested even by the arbitration community.[95]

---

[91] Although an appeals facility was negotiated on these IIAs, they were never implemented.

[92] *Model Text for the Indian Bilateral Investment Treaty*, Investment Policy Hub (2015), https://investmentpolicyhub.unctad.org/Download/TreatyFile/3560 (last visited Dec 02, 2018). "Article 29. Appeals Facility. The Parties may by agreement or after the completion of their respective procedures regarding the enforcement of this Treaty may establish an institutional mechanism to develop an appellate body or similar mechanism to review awards rendered by tribunals."

[93] *Possible Improvements of the Framework for ICSID Arbitration*, Icsid.worldbank.org (2004), https://icsid.worldbank.org/en/Documents/resources/Possible%20Improvements%20of%20the%20Framework%20of%20ICSID%20Arbitration.pdf (last visited Feb 3, 2019).

[94] *See* Feldman, *supra* note 19. *See also* Elsa Sardinha, *The Impetus for the Creation of an Appellate Mechanism*, 32 ICSID REVIEW - FOREIGN INVESTMENT LAW JOURNAL 503-527 (2017).

[95] *See* Nikos Lavranos, *supra* note 87. The European Federation for Investment

The EU also intends for its prospective MIC to possibly serve as the appeals mechanism for some countries that might prefer to settle their investment disputes within the current *ad hoc* system, but nevertheless might want the opportunity to review the decisions it issues. In a paper submitted to WG III in January 2019, where the EU outlines its proposal to establish a permanent Multilateral Investment Court, it proposes an open architecture scheme that ensures a certain level of flexibility to accommodate the interests of such countries.[96]

Theoretically, the establishment of an appeals mechanism would have the advantage of addressing some of the main concerns over the ISDS, while avoiding the abovementioned practical difficulties of an ICS and resistance from stakeholders interested in maintaining the *status quo*. Moreover, it would provide an alternative way to ensure the correctness of arbitral awards and promote the emergence of a consistent set of rules through the repeated examination of similar cases by a permanent group of judges, which is only possible when parties are required to use the same tribunal for dispute resolution.[97] By promoting consistency and predictability, and reducing the risks of conflicting decisions, an appellate mechanism could restore faith in the ISDS, thus enhancing its legitimacy and sustainability over the long term.

Whereas an appeals mechanism would maintain some of the main features of the *ad hoc* regime, it would drastically change other characteristics that have been portrayed as big advantages of the current ISDS. While appellate review could provide an alternative way of ensuring the integrity of arbitral awards, it could also severely undermine some of the great merits of the current

---

Law and Arbitration (EFILA), reacting to the European proposal to establish an ICS during the TTIP negotiations, suggested that "the US and the EU should also consider whether it would not be more preferable to modify and Improve existing systems, such as turning the ICSID annulment procedure into a full appeal mechanism."

[96] Submission establishing a standing mechanism for the settlement of international investment disputes, Trade.ec.europa.eu, at 9 (2019), http://trade.ec.europa.eu/doclib/html/157631.htm (last visited Feb 11, 2019).

[97] *See* Eric A. Posner & John C. Yoo, *Judicial Independence in International Tribunals*, 93 CALIFORNIA LAW REVIEW, at 24 (2005).

ISDS, which are efficiency and finality.[98] Besides that, as emphasized in the previous section, it is expected that parties would face extra costs and more delays in an appeals system, as it is reasonable to assume that it would be frequently invoked by the losing parties.

c. ICSID Reform—The Establishment Strikes Back

The ICSID was established in 1966 and is the world's leading institution dedicated to international investment dispute settlement, having administered the majority of all international investment disputes, which amounts to more than 600 cases to date.[99] The ICSID Convention, Regulations, and Rules are frequently subject to improvements and have already been amended to address concerns over transparency, independence, the impartiality of arbitrators, and time effectiveness.[100]

In the realm of the current ISDS crisis, the ICSID Secretariat initiated consultations in late 2016 with its Member States and the general public to identify areas where further reform might be needed. A similar invitation was issued to the public in early 2017. This marks the fourth rule-amendment process and is the most extensive review to date.[101] The stated goals of this review are to modernize, simplify and streamline the rules, while also reducing the environmental footprint of ICSID proceedings. However, the process of consultation with Member States and the public resulted in 16 areas for potential amendments, which coincide with several areas for possible improvement already identified by UNCITRAL

---

[98] *See* Ian Laird & Rebecca Askew, *Finality Versus Consistency: Does Investor-State Arbitration Need an Appellate System*, 7 THE JOURNAL OF APPELLATE PRACTICE AND PROCESS, AT 298 (2005),
http://lawrepository.ualr.edu/appellatepracticeprocess/vol7/iss2/9 (last visited Jan 25, 2019).
[99] *See* ICSID, Icsid.worldbank.org (2018),
https://icsid.worldbank.org/en/Pages/about/default.aspx (last visited Jan 25, 2019).
[100] ICSID Amendments, Icsid.worldbank.org (2018),
https://icsid.worldbank.org/en/amendments/Pages/About/about.aspx (last visited Jan 25, 2019).
[101] *Id.*

WG III.[102]

The EU's proposal to establish a two-tier tribunal with a permanent body of adjudicators and an appellate body is a radical departure from the existing ISDS regime. The creation of such a tribunal, with a significant support among states, would be a major threat to the ICSID's existence.[103] Therefore, the launch of such an extensive review process by the ICSID seems to indicate that the ICSID Secretariat is concerned about a radical reshaping of the ISDS regime that could be harmful to its own existence. It is also an indication that the ICSID is not willing to participate in the EU's initiative. Instead, such an initiative shows that the ICSID

---

[102] List of Topics for Potential ICSID Rule Amendment, Icsid.worldbank.org (2018), https://icsid.worldbank.org/en/Documents/about/List of Topics for Potential ICSID Rule Amendment-ENG.pdf (last visited Jan 25, 2019). The potential areas for amendment of ICSID rules are: 1. Review Procedure for Appointment and Disqualification of Arbitrators, Explore Feasibility of Code of Conduct for Arbitrators, 2. Clarify Rules on Preliminary Objections and Bifurcation 3. Explore Possible Provisions on Consolidation of Proceedings and Parallel Proceedings 4. Modernize Institution Rules, Means of Communications and Filing of Briefs and Supporting Documentation, and General Functions of the Secretariat 5. Modernize and Simplify Rules concerning the First Session, Procedural Consultation and Pre-Hearing Conference 6. Modernize Rules on Witnesses and Experts and Other Evidence 7. Explore Possible Provisions for Suspension of Proceedings and Clarify Rules on Discontinuance when Parties Fail to Act 8. Reflect Best Practices for Preparation of Award, Separate and Dissenting Opinions 9. Explore Presumption in Favor of Allocating Costs to the Prevailing party, Possible Provisions on Security for Costs and Security for Stay of Enforcement of Awards 10. Review Provisions on Provisional Measures 11. Clarify and Streamline Procedure in Annulment Proceedings 12. Review and Modernize Provisions on Costs, Fees and Payment of Advances, and Discontinuance for Failure to Pay Advances 13. Explore Possible Provisions on Transparency, Clarify Rules on Non-Disputing party Participation 14. Improve Time and Cost Efficiency and Explore Feasibility of Guide for Efficient Conduct of Process 15. Explore Possible Provisions on Third party Funding 16. Streamline Additional Facility Rules for Non-ICSID Convention Cases.

[103] Notwithstanding the natural outcome of the ICS's success being the decline in ICSID's membership, there are still legal options for the ICSID to participate in the EU's initiative, either by providing administrative support, serving as a forum for negotiations, or even serving as the organization onto which the new mechanism might be docked. See N. Jansen Calamita, *The Challenge of Establishing a Multilateral Investment Tribunal at ICSID*, 32 ICSID REVIEW 611-624 (2017).

strives for the continuity of the current regime and aims to solve the concerns that gave rise to dissatisfaction with the ISDS.

ICSID's Effort to Improve Consistency

Much has been discussed about the ability of *ad hoc* tribunals to enhance the consistency of awards. Despite ICSID tribunals using *ad hoc* arbitration to settle international investment disputes on the basis of heterogeneous treaty provisions, there is a tendency among ICSID tribunals to develop a homogeneous methodology regarding international law.[104] However, ICSID could do significantly more to enhance the consistency of the awards issued by its numerous tribunals.[105]

In the current amendment process, ICSID is innovating by introducing options for the consolidation and coordination of claims.[106] The consolidation proceedings include the appointment of the same arbitrators to hear otherwise separate cases, organizing joint hearings, or ensuring that the awards are rendered simultaneously. The consolidation of claims tends to reduce the costs of proceedings and improve the consistency of the awards in cases where the background of the disputes is identical or similar. This novelty in the ICSID Arbitration Rules replicates some provisions on the consolidation and coordination of claims already in place for the permanent courts recently negotiated by the European Union.[107]

Moreover, some of the proposed rules aimed at enhancing transparency indirectly help to prevent inconsistencies. The proposed AR 48, which regulates the submission of non-disputing parties (NDP), states in its paragraph five, that "the Tribunal may provide the NDP with access to relevant documents filed in the

---

[104] Ole Kristian Fauchald, *The Legal Reasoning of ICSID Tribunals - An Empirical Analysis*, 19 EUROPEAN JOURNAL OF INTERNATIONAL LAW 301-364 (2008).
[105] *Id.*
[106] *See* Proposals for Amendment of the ICSID Rules — Working Paper, Icsid.worldbank.org (2018), https://icsid.worldbank.org/en/Documents/Amendments_Vol_3_Complete_WP+Schedules.pdf (last visited Jan 26, 2019), AR 38 and 38 bis.
[107] *See* article 8.43.1 of CETA. *See also* article 3.59.1 of the EU – Vietnam FTA.

proceeding, unless either party objects."[108] By allowing the tribunal to order the production of case documents, the parties would better understand case law, focus their arguments more precisely, and predict likely outcomes more accurately. The parties and their legal counsel would be able to enhance their comprehension of similar provisions in other cases. Over time, the disclosure of case law documents would be expected to produce more predictability and consequently more consistent awards.

Revision, Annulment and the Trade-off Between Finality and Correctness

Whereas the ICS discussions on addressing the limited mechanisms to ensure correctness of awards include establishing an appellate tribunal with the competence to review first-instance awards, the ICSID's proposed amendment only aims at streamlining the rules of procedures governing the interpretation, revision, and annulment of awards, as well as codifying ICSID practices, in relation to post-award remedy proceedings.[109]

A more comprehensive reform aimed at ensuring the correctness of tribunal awards, such as the establishment of an appellate body in the ICSID framework, has proved very difficult in the past. Criticisms of these changes range from a loss of finality to the increased cost and duration of ISDS proceedings. Therefore, it is expected that a possible outcome of the current reform, in this regard, would not include comprehensive changes to the current rules. Instead, the proposals unveiled so far show a preference for the improvement of existing mechanisms, rather than the creation of broader mechanisms for the revision and annulment of awards.[110]

---

[108] *See* Proposals for Amendment of the ICSID Rules — Working Paper, *supra* note 104, at 212-13.

[109] *See id.*, at 270.

[110] It is important to emphasize that the ICSID has received several comments on this issue during the process of consultation with its Member States and the public. A noteworthy opinion from a law firm argues for the necessity of a collegial body to scrutinize awards in order to pressure the tribunal to keep the quality and timing of awards acceptable. According to the commentators, there is a considerable and growing disparity in this regard, which is reinforced by the

Addressing Independence and Impartiality While Maintaining the *Status Quo*

ICSID amendment proposals also envisage addressing the issue of independence and impartiality of adjudicators. The proposed changes do not abandon the current scheme of party appointment, and instead only improve certain provisions that could affect the arbitrators' independence and impartiality. The process of challenging arbitrators, for example, has been revised, including the introduction of an expedited schedule for parties filing a challenge, as well as an enhanced declaration of independence and impartiality.[111] Moreover, ICSID together with UNCITRAL Secretarial are working on a Code of Conduct for arbitrators aimed at ensuring the consistency of ethical requirements across all the major sets of rules used for ISDS.[112] Once final, this Code of Conduct would be added as an amendment to the ICSID rules.

Furthermore, the information disclosure requirements from arbitrators appointed at the start of a case have been increased. The new declaration requires the disclosure of significant relationships within the last five years between the appointee and the parties, the parties' counsel, other members of the tribunal, third-party funders, and any involvement in other Investor-State cases, in any

---

absence of scrutiny during the enforcement stage, as well as a lack of review during the annulment stage, which could pressure tribunal members to be more attentive to quality. However, such broader suggestions have not been incorporated to the proposed rules for amendment thus far. *See* Public Comments to Amendment of ICSID's Rules and Regulations, Icsid.worldbank.org (2019),
https://icsid.worldbank.org/en/Documents/about/Public%20Comments%20to%20Amendment%20to%20ICSID%20Rules%20and%20Regulations.pdf (last visited Jan 25, 2019), at 155.

[111] *See* Backgrounder on Proposals for Amendment of the ICSID Rules, Icsid.worldbank.org (2018),
https://icsid.worldbank.org/en/Documents/Amendment_Backgrounder.pdf (last visited Jan 25, 2019).

[112] *See* Proposals for Amendment of the ICSID Rules — Synopsis, Icsid.worldbank.org, at 5 (2018),
https://icsid.worldbank.org/en/amendments/Documents/Homepage/Amendments-Vol_1_Synopsis_EN,FR,SP.pdf (last visited Jan 25, 2019).

capacity.113 Those are clearly provisions aimed at reducing the chances of double-hatting and will likely prevent conflicts of interest during the selection process by providing the parties with more complete information on how to instruct a disqualification claim.

The proposed rules, however, do not intend to prohibit double-hatting, but only to provide more detailed information to assess whether a *de facto* conflict exists.114 Instead, their aim is to enhance transparency and enable parties to consider potential conflicts of interest derived from double-hatting on a case-by-case basis.115

Transparency of Proceedings

The current amendment process includes several provisions aimed at increasing the transparency of proceedings. The relations between parties and third-party funders, which have long been an issue of concern in the current system, are further codified to introduce an obligation to the parties to disclose whether they have third-party funding, along with the source of that funding.116 The identity of the funder is required to be disclosed to potential arbitrators before their appointment, to avoid conflicts of interest. Once more, the proposed rules demonstrate the preference for a less dramatic departure from the existing rules, opting for

---

113 *See* Proposals for Amendment of the ICSID Rules — Working Paper, *supra* note 104, AR 26.

114 These options tend to preserve the interest of those individuals who frequently act in more than one of such capacities. In its submission to ICSID, Derains & Gharavi International, which "is a network bringing together lawyers who frequently act as arbitrator, counsel and consultant before tribunals" argues that a more restrictive rule in this regard would bring several drawbacks, such as reducing the pool of available ICSID arbitrators. Moreover, they argue, the arbitrator's previous experience as counsel is beneficial to the system, as their practical experience has great value when facing procedural or substantive issues. Furthermore, those arbitrators that act as counsel are less likely to be dependent on future appointments and the risks associated therewith. See Public Comments to Amendment of ICSID's Rules and Regulations, *supra* note 108, at 150.

115 *See* Proposals for Amendment of the ICSID Rules — Working Paper, *supra* note 104, at 361.

116 *See id.*, AR 21.

enhanced transparency through the mandatory disclosure of information, rather than the prohibition of third-party funding.

The proposed AR 57 aims for a greater participation of non-disputing parties (NDP). The possibility for NDPs to make written submissions has existed in the ICSID rules since 2006. The changes, however, incorporate new provisions based on practice and experience to date and are meant to further codify NDP participation.[117]

AR 57(5) would allow the tribunal to order the NDPs to have access to relevant documents filed in the proceedings. Nonetheless, the parties would still be capable of preventing the NDP from accessing any document that they might classify as confidential.[118] The novelties include additional criteria for consideration when determining whether to allow written submissions from an NDP, such as the identification of its activity or any affiliation with a disputing party, and whether the NDP has received any assistance with its filing. This will allow the tribunal to better assess whether there are any relationships between the NDP and a party.

The amendments also impose the obligation on the parties to inform whether they have third-party funding, the source of the funding, as well as the requirement of keeping such disclosures updated throughout the proceeding.[119] As highlighted above, the proposed rules also state that the name of the funder would have to be provided to the arbitrators prior to their appointment to avoid inadvertent conflicts of interest. Third-party funding is a long-

---

[117] Although that can be interpreted as an effort to enhance transparency, it is noteworthy that the ICSID has received submissions from organizations linked with the arbitration industry suggesting the adoption of tougher rules regarding *amicus curiae* submissions. The European Federation for Investment Law and Arbitration (EFILA) suggests including the possibility for the tribunal to request that an *amicus* provide security for the parties' reasonable costs in commenting on the submission of the *amicus* as a condition for allowing the *amicus* to make a submission. See Public Comments to Amendment of ICSID's Rules and Regulations, *supra* note 108, at 103.

[118] *See* Proposals for Amendment of the ICSID Rules — Working Paper, *supra* note 104, AR 57 (5).

[119] *See id.*, AR 21.

standing concern that is thought to exacerbate pathologies in the system by fueling speculative claims, as well as asymmetric operation in favor of claimants.[120] Despite all the criticism, the current amendment process, once more, opts for adopting a remedy to its deficiencies rather than a complete prohibition of third-party funding.

The consent of both parties to publish an award would still be mandatory under the ICSID Convention—that remains unchanged. However, the proposed AR 44(2) states that consent to publish an award would be deemed to have been given if a party has not objected to it, in writing, within 60 days.[121] Even if a party objects, the proposed rules would permit the ICSID to publish legal excerpts of the award, leaving the requirement undisturbed. Therefore, although the proposed rules would remain largely similar to the existing ones, transparency would be fostered, as the publication of the award would come to be the general rule, rather than the exception.[122]

Amendments Envisaged to Reduce the Costs of the Proceedings

The ICSID amendments regarding financial provisions also reflect the concerns over the increasing costs of ISDS proceedings. The proposed rules would modify the current one to entitle members to a fixed fee, measured only by hours of work, rather than the current method of a flat daily fee irrespective of the number of hours worked during the hearings.[123] The new rule unifies the fee structure, so that all work performed is compensated transparently, equally and exactly. Moreover, the proposed rule

---

[120] *See* Howse, *supra* note 35.
[121] *See* Proposals for Amendment of the ICSID Rules — Working Paper, *supra* note 104, AR 44 (2).
[122] Corroborating the view that enhanced transparency can improve the development of consistent case law, the EFILA contends "that where ICSID Secretariat is prevented from publishing such a decision or order due to lack of party consent, it should have the power to publish extracts, if it considers them important for the development of international law." See Public Comments to Amendment of ICSID's Rules and Regulations, *supra* note 108, at 103.
[123] *See* Proposals for Amendment of the ICSID Rules — Working Paper, *supra* note 104, AFR 7.

states that all filings would have to be done electronically, unless there are special reasons to maintain paper filing,[124] in an attempt to make the processes faster and less expensive.[125] Notwithstanding the merits of this modification, its impact on the overall cost of the ISDS proceedings would not be significant.[126]

Furthermore, requests by tribunal members to be paid more than the ICSID fee (currently $3,000/day) are further regulated by Administrative Financial Regulation (AFR) 14. The proposed amendments would simplify the financial administration of proceedings, while ensuring that costs are transparent, predictable, and fair.[127] It therefore would contribute to keeping the parties' expenditures under their control.

AR 19 proposes another modification aimed at reducing the costs of proceedings. It encourages tribunals to make cost orders on an interim basis and not just in the final award, to keep parties cost-conscious during the interlocutory stage and to help parties to gauge the ongoing costs of a case.[128] As a result it may encourage parties to refrain from continuing cases that could give rise to further adverse cost orders.[129]

New Time Limits to Expedite Cases

Another major criticism of the ISDS that the current ICSID amendment process also addresses is the increasing duration of proceedings. The amendment rules set clearer and realistic timeframes and implement options for expedited proceedings, featuring additional and shortened timelines. The proposed AR 59

---

[124] *See id.*, AR 3 (1).
[125] *See* Backgrounder on Proposals for Amendment of the ICSID Rules, *supra* note 109, at 2.
[126] This is the authors' own assessment. We assume that merely replacing the 'flat daily fee' rule to a criterion that measure by hours do very few to reduce the enormous costs with legal counsel. Likewise, by replacing paper filling by electronic filling has almost 0 effect on reducing costs.
[127] *See* Proposals for Amendment of the ICSID Rules — Working Paper, *supra* note 104, AFR 14.
[128] *See id.*, AR 19.
[129] *See* Proposals for Amendment of the ICSID Rules — Synopsis, *supra* note 110, at 4.

sets clear expectations for tribunal members to render the award in a timely manner, while maintaining flexibility, based on individual circumstances of each case.[130] It revises the current AR 46, which deals with the preparation and timing of the award.[131] Under the current rule, the award must be rendered within 120 days after the close of the proceedings. However, since tribunals normally do not close the proceedings until the award is almost finalized, this provision rarely limits the time for deciding a case.[132]

The latest available numbers on ICSID arbitration proceedings demonstrate that the average duration, from the registration of the case until the rendering of the award, is approximately 49 months.[133] The proposed AR 59 states that awards must be rendered within 60 days after the last submission of an application for manifest lack of legal merit, 180 days after the last submission on a preliminary objection, and 240 days after the last submission on all ancillary matters.[134]

However, it is important to emphasize that the 240-day limit is a "best-efforts" obligation under the proposed AR 8(3).[135] Therefore, the amendments seek to ensure that awards be issued more expeditiously and under clearer time limits, based on the complexity of the case and on the amount of information it has to deal with.[136] The ICSID received numerous comments from law

---

[130] *See* Proposals for Amendment of the ICSID Rules — Working Paper, *supra* note 104, AR 59.
[131] *See* ICSID Convention, *supra* note 22, AR 46.
[132] *See* Proposals for Amendment of the ICSID Rules — Working Paper, *supra* note 104, at 257.
[133] *See id.*, at 257.
[134] *See id.*, at AR 59.
[135] Proposed AR 8 (3) states that ''Where these Rules prescribe time limits for orders, decisions and the Award, the Tribunal, or the Chairman, where applicable, shall use best efforts to meet those time limits. If special circumstances arise which prevent the Tribunal from complying with a time limit, it shall advise the parties of the reason for delay and the date when it anticipates the order, decision or Award will be delivered.'' *Id.*
[136] The ICSID's option for such lax language came despite severe criticism received during the consultation process. In this sense: ''It has become too common for extensive time to lapse, sometimes up to two years, between the hearing and the rendering of the award and to serve standard excuses, ranging from complexity of cases to dissents. In general, it should be made clear that it is

firms and arbitration associations during the consultation period. Most of the comments conveyed suggestions for normative innovations aimed at increasing efficiency and celerity in the conclusion of proceedings, which ranged from introduction of shorter timeframes[137] to best-endeavors provisions.[138] The interpretation of AR 59, alongside AR 8 (3), nonetheless makes it clear that the ICSID has opted for the "best-endeavors" language when amending its rules.

The proposed amendment introduced a new chapter with an optional expedited arbitration procedure that would significantly reduce the timeframes and complexity of proceedings.[139] Another

---

unacceptable to receive awards more than a year after the evidentiary hearing, whether or not there are post hearing briefs." Public Comments to Amendment of ICSID's Rules and Regulations, *supra* note 108, at 152.

[137] "To increase efficiency and celerity in the conclusion of proceedings, consider introducing the requirement that the proceedings be declared closed within a specific time period from the end of the final hearing or the filing of the last post-hearing written submissions." *Id.*, at 200. Another comment from a law firm suggests a rule "to authorize the Secretary-General to reduce the fees of the arbitrators where, an award has not been drawn up and signed within the specified period of time after closure of the proceedings". *Id.*, at 200. Organizations linked with the arbitration community proposed that "ICSID considers issuing guidelines for limiting submission length, volume of document production, and frivolous applications, and ii) prohibition on more than one round of post-hearing submissions." *Id.*, at 194. EFILA, in turn, suggests "shortening of the deadlines envisaged in the procedure for constituting the tribunal in the absence of previous agreement." *Id.*, at 102.

[138] "To encourage time and cost efficiency, consider introducing a rule expressly adopting the general principle that the tribunal and the parties shall act in an efficient and expeditious manner" *Id.*, at 202. The "practice of informing the parties that the arbitrators' fees have been reduced due to a delay in the rendering of the award is not the correct approach. It undermines the authority of the Tribunal in its adjudicatory function. Any process for controlling the delay in rendering the award should remain confidential, and overseen by the ICSID Secretariat, potentially via the Tribunal's secretary, without opening up the issue with the Parties to the extent possible." *Id.*, at 152.

[139] Proposed rules allow the parties to expressly opt into an expedited process for the full arbitration within 20 days from the notice of registration. Under the Expedited Arbitration, the parties must select arbitrators within 30 days of registration and can opt for only one arbitrator or three-person tribunal. Under the rules of the expedited process, the first session is held within 30 days. Memorials and counter-memorials are each filed in 60 days and limited to 200

noteworthy modification aimed at reducing the duration of ISDS proceedings is the adoption of an expedited schedule for parties to challenge arbitrators. Mentioned as one of the most prominent causes for delays in the outcomes of ISDS proceedings, challenges to arbitrators are deemed to increase the length of a proceeding by 65 to 82 percent.[140] In order to make this process quicker, the proposed AR 29 would introduce an expedited schedule for parties to file a challenge.[141]

The new rules also require all arguments and supporting documents to be included in the disqualification proposal, thus transforming what could otherwise be a formally lodged challenge into a complete written submission, which reduces the overall time needed for the briefing. With the clear intention to minimize potential delays in proceedings, the proposed AR 29(3) would eliminate the automatic suspension of the proceeding upon the

---

pages, while replies and rejoinders may each be filed within 40 days and are limited to 100 pages. The hearing is held within 60 days after the last written submission. The Tribunal can extend the timetable by 30 days to address document disclosure motions, if needed. It may also adjust the schedule if needed for preliminary objection or ancillary claim, but retaining the expedited nature of the process. *See* Proposals for Amendment of the ICSID Rules — Working Paper, *supra* note 104, AR 69-79.

[140] This statistic comes from research being conducted by Pluricourts. Though it is not yet finished, the data was unveiled by the delegate of Pluricourts present at the thirty-sixth meeting of UNCITRAL Working Group III, during the session that discussed the concerns of cost and duration of ISDS proceedings on 01\11\2018 during the afternoon. See Malcolm Langford, UNCITRAL WG III (Investor-State Dispute Settlement Reform) - Speakers Log with Audio Recordings (2018), http://www.uncitral.org/uncitral/audio/meetings.jsp (last visited Jan 26, 2019).

[141] Under this new schedule, a specific time limit of 20 days for filing a disqualification motion replaces the former requirement that it should be filed "promptly." The challenge may be proposed any time before the award is rendered, since it is made within 20 days after the date on which the party first knew or first should have known of the facts on which the proposal is based. The disqualifications proceeding follows with a reply by the responding party that is filed in seven days, then arbitrator observation within further five days. After that, the parties shall file final observations simultaneously within seven days. Finally, the decision is rendered in 30 days. See Proposals for Amendment of the ICSID Rules — Working Paper, *supra* note 104, AR 29.

filing of a challenge.[142] It gives the parties the ability to decide whether the proceeding will be suspended while the disqualification procedure is pending.

IV. CONCLUSION

The crisis in the ISDS system has reached a stage in which most of its users agree that the system urgently requires reform. While a consensus exists on this necessity, the regulatory options and institutional reforms are still under discussion. So far, three options have taken shape and gained relevance in international debate.

The creation of an ICS in the form of a two-tier tribunal, composed of permanent and financially independent adjudicators with fixed terms, is the most radical departure from the existing system and its successful implementation could pose a major threat to the *ad hoc* ISDS. Although this option presents the best way to address the most remarkable flaws of the ISDS, it also contains several drawbacks in comparison with the current *ad hoc* system, and its implementation presents several practical difficulties.

The simple creation of an appellate body that would be responsible for reviewing the *ad hoc* tribunals' awards responds to only one part of the criticism faced by the ISDS. It neglects other serious problems such as the issue of party appointment and its effect on the independence and impartiality of arbitrators. This alternative implies curtailing some of the most heralded advantages of the ISDS—namely the celerity of the proceedings and the finality of the tribunal awards—but nonetheless leaves the *ad hoc* system unchanged and would thus reduce resistance from the arbitration industry.

Finally, the reform of the current system, represented here by the ICSID amendment process, envisages maintaining the *status quo* and making simple cosmetic changes. Arguments in favor of maintaining the *status quo* are that overhead costs that do not currently exist would not be created and that it promotes an

---

[142] *See id.*, AR 29 (3).

equilibrium between the rights and interests of investors and states, as opposed to the ICS proposal, which critics say would eventually prevent investors from participating in the composition of tribunals.

The trade-off between the three reform options is clear. All of them have advantages and disadvantages, and discussions about the most appropriate alternative to solve the current crisis is likely to last for years. Nevertheless, discussion on this topic is welcome at this time of grave discontent with the current investment dispute resolution regime. With multiple ISDS reform initiatives ongoing, policymaking in this area is in its most ebullient phase. The next developments will demonstrate the measure of success of each alternative. The preference of the countries for each model will reveal whether any of the three paradigms will prevail or if the investment dispute resolution regime will embrace the coexistence of more than one paradigm.

WHEN PEER PRESSURE IS NOT ENOUGH: MANDATORY DISCLOSURE AND THIRD-PARTY FUNDING

Sarah Gilcrest

I. Introduction

While the rise of third-party funding agreements helped parties arbitrate their claims without harming their bottom lines, there is a high potential for unforeseen conflicts of interest to arise. The arbitral community is fairly small, with arbitrators having repeat appointments, counsel representing various parties, and funders pulling the purse strings.

This paper defines a conflict of interest within a third-party funding context and takes a look at why mandatory disclosure is important for the future of third-party funding and the arbitration community as a whole. It also analyzes the role states can play in supporting the legitimacy of arbitration through legislation. Of course, legislation is not necessarily the quickest method, but it is the most enforceable. The arbitral community should lean on the enforceability of hard law to require mandatory disclosure of the existence and identity of third-party funders. Requiring parties to disclose funding not only helps avoid conflicts of interest throughout an arbitration, but it can also lead to more enforceable awards and increase participation and trust in the system, while still maintaining the confidentiality of the process.

In this paper, I explain the mechanics of third-party funding and the types of funders who provide monetary support to claims. Second, I explain the types of conflicts that can arise when third party funding is involved in a dispute, and better define what a conflict of interest actually means within a third-party funding context. Finally, I argue that requiring parties to disclose the name and existence of any funder throughout the course of an arbitration can help avoid conflicts throughout the process, lead to greater enforceability, and increase participation and trust in the arbitral process.

II. What is Third-Party Funding and Who Are These Funders?

This paper adopts the following definition and description of third-party funding loosely based off the definition provided in the Queen Mary Report: third-party funding is when a party (generally the claimant, but in a small number of cases, the respondent), an affiliate of the party, or the law firm representing that party funds a claim by receiving financial support from a third-party financial institution.[1] These arrangements either come in the form of equity or debt instruments, full or partial transfer of the claim, and risk avoidance instruments.[2] These are large loans that can cover legal fees, administrative costs, expert fees, or even the business operating expenses of the party.[3] A particular feature of these loans is that they are non-

---

[1] Report of the ICCA-Queen Mary Task Force on Third-Party Funding in International Arbitration, The ICCA Reports No. 4 92 (April 2018) (The term "third-party funder" refers to any natural or legal person who is not a party to the dispute and is not a party's legal counsel, but who enters into an agreement either with a party, an affiliate of that party, or a law firm representing that party: (a) In order to provide material support for or to finance part or all of the cost of the proceedings, either individually or as part of a specific range of cases, and; (b) Such support or financing is provided through a donation, or grant, or in exchange for remuneration or reimbursement wholly or partially dependent on the outcome of the dispute).
[2] Burcu Osmanoglu, *Third-Party Funding in International Commercial Arbitration and Arbitrator Conflict of Interest*, 32 J. Int'l Arb. 325, 329 (2015).
[3] Yves Derains, *Foreword to Third-Party Funding in International Arbitration*, ICC Dossier No. 752E, 5 (2013).

recourse, meaning that if the claimant or respondent is unsuccessful, they do not have to repay the funder.[4]

The International Bar Association (IBA) 2014 Guidelines on Conflicts of Interests[5] defines third-party funding as "any person or entity that is contributing funds or material support to the prosecution or defense of the case and that has a direct economic interest in the award to be rendered in the arbitration."[6] This excludes other types of funding like bank loans, intra-group financing, and philanthropic financing from non-governmental organizations.[7]

Third-party funders can either specifically focus on third-party funding or use this type of financial instrument as a way to diversify their portfolios.[8] Generally these specialized firms are in countries with well-developed third-party funding industries and legal systems like Australia, Germany, the United Kingdom, and the United States.[9]

III. What is a Conflict of Interest?

The rise of third-party funding in arbitration and the small community of arbitrator-lawyers can create a perfect

---

[4] Jennifer A. Trusz, Note, *Full Disclosure? Conflicts of Interest Arising from Third-Party Funding in International Commercial Arbitration*, 101 Geo. L.J., 1649, 1653 (2013).
[5] Hereinafter the "IBA Guidelines".
[6] IBA Guidelines on Conflicts of Interest in International Arbitration, 13 (adopted Oct. 23, 2014) (updated Aug. 5, 2015) (citing Explanation of General Standard 6(b)).
[7] *Id.*
[8] Victoria Shannon Sahani, Lisa Bench Nieuwveld, *Third-Party Funding in International Arbitration* 3, 1-20 (2d ed. 2017), https://ssrn.com/abstract=3046300 (noting Chapter 1: Introduction to Third-Party Funding).
[9] *Id.*, at 3.

storm of conflict of interest issues between the parties and the arbitrator. For example, if a party appointed arbitrator has had extensive dealings with a funder or has a financial stake in the funder's business dealings, this could negate the neutrality of the tribunal as one of the arbitrators is predisposed to favor a funded party. Or at least, set the tribunal's decision up for an impartiality challenge. Unfortunately, trying to asses a "conflict of interest" and whether that conflict could impact the tribunal's decision-making abilities is a difficult process because there is no one universal definition. Neither institution rules nor state legislation truly define when conflicts arise, and under what circumstances. Instead, they suggest guidelines, possible situations to look out for, and what type of test to apply when analyzing conflicts issues. This is helpful but offers about as much clarity as a partially fogged mirror.

Taking into account the difficulty of truly figuring out whether a conflict of interest strongly influences an arbitrator's impartial decision-making capabilities (for better or worse, individuals in society cannot read minds), I propose the following standard based off institutional guidelines, existing case law regarding arbitrator impartiality challenges, and national legislation:

> **A conflict of interest arises when there is a direct and dependent relationship between the funder and the arbitrator where the outcome of the case *significantly* affects: (1) the financial performance, profitability, or share price of the funder, or (2) the arbitrator's personal financial interests.**

This definition of a conflict of interest within a third-party funding context will not only be used as a reference point for the rest of the paper but should be adopted as the standard when analyzing third party funding conflicts. This is because it is just narrowly tailored enough to apply to the nuanced relationship between funders and tribunals, but it also sets itself up for application in existing litmus tests used by institutions and states.

Arbitral and other legal institutions (like the IBA), while great in many ways, have largely refrained from adopting one uniform definition of a conflict of interest. Instead, they just generally support the idea of an objective test. UNCITRAL for instance, in trying to define what an impartial and independent arbitrator can mean, explains that "impartiality" is a subjective test, regarding the arbitrator's state of mind, whereas "independence" is an objective test that looks to the arbitrator's relationships with the parties or funders.[10] This is why the IBA Guidelines also adopt a reasonableness test. The IBA Guidelines explain standards for what constitutes a reasonable doubt regarding an arbitrator's potential for bias and a possible test for disqualification. General Standard 2(c) states:

> "Doubts are justifiable if a reasonable third person, having knowledge of the relevant facts and circumstances, would reach the conclusion that there is a likelihood that the arbitrator may be influenced by factors other than the merits of the

---

[10] *See, e.g.*, Blackaby Nigel et al., *Redfern and Hunter on International Arbitration* ¶ 4.77, 1028 (6th ed. 2015); Fouchard, *Gaillard, Goldman on International Commercial Arbitration*, ¶ 1028 (Emmanuel Gaillard & John Savage eds., 1999); Amelie Abt, Arbitration in Germany: The Model Law Practice § 1036 at 25, (Karl-Heinz Bockstiegel, Stefan Kroll, Patricia Nacimiento eds., 2d. ed. 2015) (for German arbitration law); 50 para. 7; Judgement of 10 June 2004, *Bargues Agro Industrie SA v. Young Pecan Cie,*, XXX YB Comm. Arb. 499, 503 (Paris Cour d'appel) (2005) (for French arbitration law); Judgement of 27 June 2012, *X. v. Y. Inc., Swiss Federal Tribunal*, 4A_54/2012 ¶ 2.2.1. (for Swiss arbitration law).

case as presented by the parties in reaching his or her decision."[11]

General Standard 3(a) outlines a test for disqualification, but only when testing for the *appearance* or likelihood of bias. It uses an objective standard with a high threshold to prove.[12] Fortunately, in an effort to prove *some* sort of more substantial guidance on what could be a conflict of interest, the IBA has created red, orange, and green lists with red meaning a high likelihood of bias, orange meaning a medium likelihood of bias, and green meaning a low likelihood of bias. Generally, the list equates a higher likelihood of bias with: (1) the closeness of a relationship between an arbitrator, the party, an affiliate of the party, or the law firm (2) financial interest in the outcome of the claim; and (3) the length of the relationship between the arbitrator and the party, an affiliate of the party, or the law firm.

The red list is separated into two categories: non-waivable and waivable situations. Non-waivable situations include: the arbitrator being a manager, director, or member of the supervisory board, having a controlling influence on one of the parties or an affiliate, having a "significant financial or personal interest in the outcome," or regularly advising the party and its affiliate, of which they derive "significant financial income." "Waivable" offenses include situations where the arbitrator has relationship to the dispute (whether through prior involvement or given legal advice on the dispute to a party or affiliate), they have a direct or indirect interest in the dispute, or there is a current and slightly substantial relationship to one of the

---

[11] IBA Guidelines on Conflicts of Interest in International Arbitration, 13 (adopted Oct. 23. 2014) (updated Aug. 5, 2015) (citing General Standard 2(c)).
[12] *See id.* (citing General Standard 3(a)).

parties, or its affiliates. The orange list is similar to the waivable red list offenses, but only takes into account small services or relationships within the past three years. Green includes situations where the arbitrator has previously expressed legal opinions, currently renders services for one of the parties, or has contacts (rather than a relationship) with another arbitrator or with counsel for one of the parties.

Recently, the ICC released a "guidance note" regarding arbitrator conflicts of interest. [13] According to the President of the ICC's International Court of Arbitration, Alexis Mourré, the note is aimed at "ensuring that arbitrators are forthcoming and transparent in their disclosure of potential conflicts."[14] It does not address third-party funding specifically, but defines one potential conflict of interest as having a "business relationship." Thus, it can inferred that an arbitrator having a business relationship with an affiliate or a personal interest of any nature can include a significant financial interest in the outcome of the case could have a potential conflict of interest.

Fortunately, there are some ICSID cases that shed light

---

[13] Burcu Osmanoglu, *Third- Party Funding in International Commercial Arbitration and Arbitrator Conflict of Interest*, 32 J. Int'l Arb. 325, 348 (2015) ("According to unconfirmed information, the ICC is considering including third-party in funding in its arbitration rules.") (while it is generally frowned upon to base an argument off of rumors in an academic research paper, it looks like the rumors published in this article came to fruition as evidenced by the ICC's guidance note released in 2018 advising parties on potential conflicts arising from the use of third-party funding).

[14] International Court of Arbitration, *Note to Parties and Arbitral Tribunals on the Conduct of the Arbitration Under the ICC Rules of Arbitration* (2019), https://cdn.iccwbo.org/content/uploads/sites/3/2017/03/icc-note-to-parties-and-arbitral-tribunals-on-the-conduct-of-arbitration.pdf. (Quoting Alexis Mourre).

on how tribunals have attempted to define conflicts of interest regarding third party funding. For the most part, these cases have used an objective test to evaluate based on a "reasonable evaluation of the evidence by a third-party."[15] The subjective belief of the requesting party is not enough to satisfy the requirements of the convention.[16]

For instance, an arbitrator simply being in a leadership position as a funder is not enough to merit a successful claim of arbitrator bias. In *Suez Vivendi v. Argentina*,[17] Argentina challenged the Claimant's arbitrator appointment because it believed that her position as a board member of UBS was enough to violate the neutrality requirement. The council applied an objective standard – stating that the subjective belief of the requesting party is not enough to satisfy the requirements of the convention. And that as a result of the relationship between an arbitrator and a funder, a manifest lack of independence and impartiality of judgment must be demonstrated to a reasonable person. They looked at the following elements to determine whether a reasonable person would think that the challenged arbitrator could be biased: (1) proximity of the connection between the challenged arbitrator and the party; (2) intensity and frequency of the interactions between the challenged arbitrator and the party; (3) dependence of the challenged arbitrator on the party; (4) materiality of the benefits accruing to the challenged arbitrator as a result of the alleged connection.

Applying this four-prong test to analyze the proximity and type of relationship between the arbitrator and the

---

[15] *Suez, Sociedad General De Aguas De Barcelona, S.A. and Vivendi Universal, S.A. v. Argentina Republic*, ICSID Case No. ARB/03/199 (Investment disputes).
[16] *Id.*
[17] *Id.*

funder, the tribunal concluded that simply holding an advisory position on a large multi-national bank is not enough to disqualify an arbitrator. It is not about the type of relationship, but the closeness and influence the funder and arbitrator might exercise over the other. The tribunal ruled that "any connection between Prof. Kaufmann and the Claimants is remote and certainly not direct" because her directorship at UBS was merely supervisory and had no involvement in the day-to-day management of the corporation. Regarding element (2), there was no interaction at all between Prof. Kaufmann and the Claimants because of her UBS directorship. Regarding element (3), the tribunal said, "Prof. Kaufmann derives no benefits or advantages from and is in no way dependent on the Claimants as a result of the alleged connection." Further, "UBS shareholdings in Claimant are not material to UBS financial performance, profitability, or share price and in no way affect the compensation that Professor Kaufmann earns as a director of UBS." As a result, Prof. Kaufmann's directorship did not create a manifest lack of independence and impartiality of judgment. Even multiple appointments are not enough to give a reasonable third-party an appearance of bias. There must be a relationship of dependence.[18] This decision further illustrates that the relationship between funders and arbitrators can be complex and nuanced. Mandatory disclosure of the existence of any type of funder can help prevent challenges from being raised after the tribunal's decision has been made, because it requires the parties to continuously do a conflicts-check. However, creating an institutional

---

[18] *Universal Compression v. Venezuela*, ICSID Case No. ARB/10/9 ("Prof. Stern indicates that she has been appointed multiple times by various law firms, but that a relationship of dependence, which could endanger her independence or impartiality, does not exist here or elsewhere.").

guideline is not enough – the arbitral community must look at national legislation as well.

While institutional guidelines and arbitral decisions are important to look at to understand general trends and interpretations of guidelines, it is still important to note that they are not legally binding as national legislation. National legislation of the "big" arbitral seats (United States, United Kingdom, France, Switzerland, Hong Kong, and Singapore),[19] also outlines tests for impartiality. The Federal Arbitration Act requires parties to establish "evident partiality" to succeed in challenging an award.[20] However, there is no set standard regarding "evident partiality."[21] England and Wales do not have a statutory definition regarding arbitrator impartiality, but have developed a test through case law calling for the arbitrator to use a "state of mind which is free from any influences extraneous to the merits which is capable of dispassionate inquiry and an objective judgment, and which is not turned aside by any motivation to favour one side as against the other."[22] Case law goes on to establish an objective test stating "whether the fair-minded and informed observer, having considered the facts, would conclude that there was a real possibility that the tribunal was biased."[23]

France also adopts a reasonableness test which aims to review *any* circumstance that may influence an arbitrator's

---

[19] Aceris Law LLC, *The Seat of Arbitration in International Commercial Arbitration* (Aug. 11, 2017), https://www.acerislaw.com/seat-arbitration-international-commercial-arbitration.
[20] Federal Arbitration Act, 9 U.S.C. §§ 201-208 (1947).
[21] *Id.*
[22] *See Roylance v. The General Medical Council* PC ([1999] 3 WLR 541).
[23] *See Porter v. Magill, HL* ([2002] 2 AC 357); see also *A & Ors v B & Anor* [2011] EWHC 2345 (Comm).

judgment and create in the minds of the parties' reasonable doubts as to his impartiality or independence. For example, in *Creighton v. Qatar*, the court stated: "it is incumbent upon the judge of the lawfulness of the arbitral award to assess the independence and impartiality of the arbitrator, by pointing out any circumstance of such a nature as to alter his/her judgment and create a reasonable doubt in the eyes of the parties on these qualities, which pertain to the very essence of arbitral function."[24]

Hong Kong is similar to England and Wales since there is no statutory definition of independence or impartiality, but it has developed a test for independence and impartiality through case law. As defined by the courts, impartiality requires a state of mind to be free from any influences "extraneous to the merits of the particular case, which is capable of dispassionate inquiry and an objective judgment, and which is not turned aside by any motivation to favor one side as against the other."[25]

Once again, case law replaces a statute in Singapore regarding a test for impartiality. First, it establishes three forms of bias: actual bias, imputed bias, or apparent bias.[26] Actual bias will clearly disqualify an arbitrator from sitting on a tribunal. Imputed bias arises when an arbitrator acts (or appears to act) in their own interest.[27] In this case, if it is proven that the arbitrator has even a pecuniary or proprietary interest in the case, disqualification is automatic

---

[24] *Creighton Limited v. Minister of Finance of Qatar and Minister of Municipal Affairs and Agriculture of Qatar*, Case No 98-19068 (Official Case No) (2000) 207 Bulletin civil I, 135 (Other Reference) ILDC 772 (FR 2000) (OUP reference).
[25] *Supra* note 23.
[26] *PT Central Investindo v Franciscus Wongso and others and another matter*, [2014] 4 SLR 978.
[27] *Id.*

without needing to establish whether there is a likelihood or suspicion of bias.[28] Finally, apparent bias is established through a reasonableness test involving a two-step inquiry.[29] First, the applicant has to establish the factual circumstances suggesting the possibility of a biased tribunal.[30] Second, the court examines whether a "hypothetical fair-minded and informed observer would view those circumstances as bearing on the tribunal's impartiality in the resolution of the dispute before it."[31]

Pursuant to section 9 of Switzerland's Arbitration Act an arbitrator shall be impartial.[32] The circumstances establishing possible partiality are outlined in the rest of the section – bearing strong resemblance to the guidelines outlined by the IBA regarding conflicts of interest.[33] The test is also objective, and the subjective impression of the parties is not decisive.[34]

Defining a conflict of interest as: "…a direct and dependent relationship between the funder and the arbitrator where the outcome of the case *significantly* affects: (1) the financial performance, profitability, or share price of the funder, or (2) the arbitrator's personal financial interests,"[35] reflects this trend towards adopting an objective test regarding impartiality. Further, it takes into

---

[28] *Id.*
[29] *Id.*
[30] *Id.*
[31] *Id.*
[32] Swiss Rules of International Arbitration, Ch. 2, Art. 9 (2012).
[33] *See* Supreme Court Decision 4A_458/2009 of 10 June 2010, ASA Bull 3/2010, p. 520; *see also* Supreme Court Decision 4A_506/2007of 20 March 2008, ASA Bull 3/2008, p. 565.
[34] Supreme Court Decision 4A_260/2017 of 27 March 2003, ATF 129 III 445, ASA Bull 3/2003, p. 601.
[35] Refer to previous discussion regarding non-waivable situations.

account the fact that arbitrators do not live on the moon.36 They are real people, who form relationships with their colleagues and have a variety of financial interests. Thus, it is important to take into consideration the specific type of relationship that exists between the funder and the arbitrator when determining a conflict of interest.

IV. Mandatory Disclosure

A. Helps Avoid Conflicts of Interest Throughout an Arbitration

By requiring parties to simply disclose the existence of third-party funding and the name of the funder at the start of the arbitration (or within a timely manner if a party secures third-party funding during the arbitration), arbitrators can make better decisions in determining their own propensity for bias, ensuring that awards are more enforceable, and increasing trust and participation in the arbitral system.

ICSID is already addressing this issue by proposing mandatory disclosure in its new proposed rules amendment.37 It imposes a new obligation on the parties to disclose "whether they have third-party funding, the source of the funding, and to keep disclosure of such information

---

36 *Suez v. Vivendia*, ICSID Case No. ARB/03/19, 18 Decision on Disqualification. ("Arbitrators are not disembodied spirits swelling on Mars, who descend to earth to arbitrate a case and then immediately return to their Martian retreat to await inertly the call to arbitrate another. Like other professionals living and working in the world, arbitrators have a variety of complex connections with all sorts of persons and institutions.")

37 ICSID Secretariat, *Proposals for Amendment of the UCSID Rules – Synopsis, International Centre for Settlement of Investment Disputes* (August 2, 2018),
https://icsid.worldbank.org/en/amendments/Documents/Homepage/Amendments-Vol_1_Synopsis_EN,FR,SP.pdf.

current through the proceeding."[38] The LCIA addresses this as well, establishing an ongoing duty to disclose information about their independence to the ICC,[39] or the LCIA registrar.[40] Other groups, like the Queen Mary Task Force are in favor of this idea. In fact, in the Queen Mary Report, it states that "There was nearly universal agreement that disclosure of the identity of a funder is necessary for an arbitrator to undertake analysis of potential conflicts of interest."[41] At least one funder has acknowledged (perhaps reluctantly) that disclosing the funding relationship can be helpful in limited circumstances.[42]

Reconciling the possibility of conflicts of interest arising from third-party funding could involve this four-part solution: (1) the inclusion of arbitrator relationships with third-party funding institutions to be relevant in determining an arbitrator's independence and impartiality;

---

[38] *Id.* ("AR 21 ((AF)AR 32) imposes a new obligation on the parties to disclose whether they have third-party funding, the source of the funding, and to keep such disclosure of information current through the proceeding. They are not required to disclose the funding agreement or its contents for this purpose. The name of an involved funder will be provided to the arbitrators prior to appointment to avoid inadvertent conflicts of interest, and the Arbitrator Declaration requires confirmation that there is no conflict with the named funder.")
[39] IBA Guidelines General Standard, *supra* note 11, art. 11(2) ("Before appointment or confirmation, a prospective arbitrator shall . . . disclose in writing to the Secretariat any facts or circumstances which might be of such a nature as to call into question the arbitrator's independence in the eyes of the parties, as well as any circumstances that could give rise to reasonable doubts as to the arbitrator's impartiality.").
[40] London Court of International Arbitration, LCIA Arbitration Rules art 5.3 (2014).
[41] The ICCA Reports, *supra* note 1, at 98.
[42] Lisa Bench Nieuwveld, *To Disclose or to not Disclose-That is the Question,* Kluwer Arb. Blog (Apr. 17, 2012), http://arbitrationblog.kluwerarbitration.com/2012/04/17/to-disclose-or-to-not-disclose-that-is-the-question/.

(2) parties to disclose to the institution that it is receiving third-party funding; (3) a confidential and automatic conflicts check done by the institution if it receives notice from a party that it is receiving funding; and (4) that the arbitral tribunal shall be prohibited from considering the existence of a third-party funding relationship when determining costs or security for costs.[43] However, simply proposing a four-part conflicts check guideline does not go far enough in establishing the teeth necessary to increase the enforceability of awards. Countries should pass legislation requiring arbitral parties to disclose the existence of funding, because the hard law support of arbitration is what makes the system work.

B. Leads to More Enforceable Awards

By ensuring that all bases were covered in determining bias, it reduces the chances of a successful challenge to the tribunal's decision. If a court sees that the arbitrator and the parties went through proper steps to make sure that all potential conflicts of interest were disclosed to the arbitrator, then it decreases the chances that a challenge will be successful.

The arbitration community also needs the backing of national legislation to add legitimacy and enforceability to these disclosure rules. Further, any case law arising out of potential mandatory disclosure legislation can provide an additional source of guidance to tribunals. Currently no national legislation about mandatory disclosure in the context of third-party funding exists.[44] While arbitration

---

[43] Trusz, *supra* note 4, at 1673.
[44] *See* Aren Goldsmith and Lorenzo Melchionda, *The ICC's Guidance Note on Disclosure and Third-Party Funding: A Step in the Right Direction*, Kluwer Arb. Blog (March 14, 2016), http://arbitrationblog.kluwerarbitration.com/2016/03/14/the-iccs-guidance-note-on-disclosure-and-third-party-funding-a-step-in-the-

exists as a way to balance the unwillingness for parties to resolve disputes in domestic courts,[45] it only works because states recognize it as a legitimate dispute resolution tool[46] and enforce arbitral judgments.[47] If arbitral judgments were largely unenforceable, the entire system would collapse. As such, the arbitration community should embrace this relationship with domestic law and lean on it to lend ensure its longevity.

Looking at the most popular seats for arbitration: the United Kingdom, France, Switzerland, Sweden, Singapore, and Hong Kong,[48] it is clear that national law recognizes the need for a check to arbitrator bias.[49] By taking an additional step to ensure that arbitrators are fully informed of any potential conflict of interest, states promote neutrality in the system and ensure that unnecessary

---

right-direction/.

[45] Erin A. O'Hara and Larry E. Ribstein, *The Law Market*, Oxford University Press (2009), at 85 ("[A]rbitration as a mechanism for enabling the parties either to defensively avoid undesirable law or to affirmatively choose the law that will govern the parties' relationship.").

[46] New York Arbitration Convention, http://www.newyorkconvention.org/countries (at least 138 countries have signed the New York Arbitration Convention, which greatly limits the ways in which a contracting state can issue an award and refuse enforceability. This was signed on June 10, 1958 at the Convention on the Recognition and Enforcement of Arbitral Awards), 21 U.S.T. 2517, T.I.A.S. No. 6997, 330 U.N.T.S. 38 [hereinafter cited as New York Convention]. Article II of the New York Convention also provides for the enforcement of agreements to arbitrate.

[47] O'Hara & Ribstein, *supra* note 46, at 95. (stating that arbitration awards may be more enforceable than court judgments rendered by courts outside the US).

[48] Federal Arbitration Act, *supra* note 21.

[49] Kluwer Arbitration, www.kluwerarbitration.com (last accessed December 20, 2018) (Impartiality data gathered using the Kluwer Arbitration Database).

challenges to awards are prevented from being brought forward.

C. Increases Participation and Trust in the System

Despite its imperfection, arbitration exists because the global community at large recognizes its importance. In an age where transactions are global, arbitration's greatest strength is its neutrality.[50] The reassurance of a "neutral, reliable, and effective dispute resolution mechanism"[51] increases the trust needed to promote investment and cross-border transactions. National legislation requiring parties to disclose the existence of third-party funding to an arbitrator reassures parties that the tribunal has considered all potential conflicts of interest. It reinforces the trust parties have placed, for decades, on the neutrality of arbitration. To emphasize this point even further, it is helpful to analyze the criticisms of mandatory disclosure.

Some argue that mandatory disclosure of third-party funding would replace independent analysis of case-by-case thinking on the relationships between arbitrators and funders,[52] that it would lead to split conflicts standards,[53] and that no one would be willing to enforce or participate in a mandatory disclosure regime – ultimately resulting in

---

[50] Jan Paulsson, *International Arbitration is Not Arbitration*, 2 Stockholm Int'l Arb.n Rev. 1, 2 (2008) ("In international arbitration, all of these elements of evaluation fade into relative insignificance when contrasted with a criterion that is dominant here although it is, by definition, irrelevant in the national context. This alone tells you that international arbitration is not arbitration. That unique criterion is neutrality.").
[51] O'Hara & Ribstein, *supra* note 46, at 97.
[52] Jonas von Goeler, Third-Party Funding in International Arbitration and its Impact on Procedure 291 (Kluwer Law International, 2016).
[53] *Id.*, at 283-84.

lower participation.[54]

Mandatory disclosure would not discourage relationships between arbitrators and funders.[55] Instead, requiring parties to disclose the existence of third-party funding would encourage arbitrators, legislators, judges, and parties to constantly evaluate relationships in the context of third-party funding. Further, striving for a degree of perceived legal certainty in complex cases regarding an extremely subjective topic is what the law does. A great example of this are the impartiality tests set forth by England[56], France[57], Hong Kong[58], Singapore,[59] Switzerland,[60] and the United States.[61] These tests set forth a legal certainty (the type of test to measure impartiality and independence) to make sense of a complex and fact-specific topic. Further, national law *requiring* parties, rather than just encouraging them through institutional peer pressure, to disclose the existence of funding, additionally encourages them to reflect on third-party funding relationships. And it still gives tribunals and courts the

---

[54] *Id.*, at 288.
[55] *Id.*, at 291 ("[S]triving for a degree of perceived legal certainty in evaluating conflicts of interest . . . would replace independent case by case thinking on relationships involving third-party funders in a complex world of business and finance.").
[56] *See Roylance v. The General Medical Council PC* ([1999] 3 WLR 541.
[57] *Creighton Limited v. Minister of Finance of Qatar and Minister of Municipal Affairs and Agriculture of Qatar*, Case No 98-19068 (Official Case No) (2000) 207 Bulletin civil I, 135 (Other Reference) ILDC 772 (FR 2000) (OUP reference).
[58] *Roylance*, *supra* note 23.
[59] *PT Central Investindo v Franciscus Wongso* and others and another matter [2014] 3 SGHC 190.
[60] Federal Supreme Court of 10 June 2010, ASA Bull 3/2010, 520 and of 20 March 2008, ASA Bull 3/2008, 565.
[61] Federal Arbitration Act, 9 U.S.C. §§ 201-208 (1947).

freedom to consider each case on its merits – which is one of the reasons why parties choose arbitration over domestic court systems.

There is also the argument that it would lead to the coexistence of different disclosure regimes creating a lack of clarity and split conflicts standards.[62] This lack of clarity would dissuade parties from participating in systems requiring mandatory disclosure because the unknown consequences of obtaining third-party funding would dissuade investors, parties, and arbitrators from engaging in arbitration.[63] National legislation requiring mandatory disclosure actually removes this "perceived" lack of clarity because of the myriad of case law parties can use as guidance when analyzing possible third-party conflicts of interest.

National legislation also helps to sidestep the resistance some parties have towards the idea that institutions, themselves, should address this issue. James Clanchy, the former registrar and deputy director of the LCIA, when asked whether arbitral institutions should shoulder the burden of clearing potential conflicts of interest between arbitrators and third-party funders, was very much against the idea.[64] He argued that it would be a terrible idea, that it would place an unrealistic burden on the institution, and that it would lead funders and clients to avoid the rules of the institution.[65] National legislation mitigates this unrealistic burden by placing the enforcement mechanism in the hands of the state. This allows arbitral institutions to

---

[62] Goeler, *supra* note 53, at 284.
[63] *Id.*
[64] *TheJudgeVideo*, IA event - Full video, Youtube (July 25, 2013), https://www.youtube.com/watch?v=cwZQvgE1tvQ&feature=youtu.be&t=3740.
[65] *Id.*

lean on state enforcement methods to require disclosure. Further, simply requiring parties to answer a yes or no question, then providing only the name of a funder does not add any more of a burden on the parties than checking a box.

Of course, some parties might seek to avoid mandatory disclosure rules and encourage states to adopt a "race to the bottom" – where disclosure is not required, and the rules are scarce. However, it is unclear what benefit a party would gain from refusing disclosure. Mandatory disclosure still protects the confidentiality of the funding agreement.

Being unwilling to disclose funding, in the hope that if they lose they could "discover" a conflict of interest between an arbitrator and funder would be a terrible idea. Considering that existing institutional and national standards for demonstrating the objective appearance of bias are so high, it is extremely unlikely that a potential challenge would pass muster. Furthermore, more regulation does not necessarily result in a marked decrease of participation.[66] In fact, in high value situations, it makes sense that parties would default to rules requiring mandatory disclosure because it increases their chance for a more enforceable award and reassures parties that a significant element in determining the existence of a conflict of interest is taken care of. Further, mandatory disclosure still protects the confidentiality of the funding agreements by prohibiting disclosure of the terms of the agreement. Further, courts have been reluctant to look at funding agreements unless the agreement itself is under scrutiny.[67] While requiring parties to give up the name of

---

[66] IBA Guidelines on Conflicts of Interest in International Arbitration, *supra* note 5.
[67] Press Release, Oxus Gold PLC, *Litigation Funding* (March 1, 2012) (Oxus issued a press release disclosing recourse to third-party funding

the funder, it still keeps the terms of the relationship confidential, reassuring funders that tribunals will not take the name of a funder into its decisions for regarding security for costs or fee shifting.[68] This incentivizes third-party funders to be more comfortable with parties disclosing the name of the funder, and can in fact, encourage parties to arbitrate in those jurisdictions because the confidential nature of their agreement can be kept intact. [69]

V. Conclusion: Third-party Funding is Here to Stay

Issues arising from third-party funding should not be ignored, not just because of the ethical implications, but also because of the sheer amount of money involved. With judgments reaching in the billions of dollars,[70] more money

---

and revealed details of the funding agreement); *Sehil v. Turkmenistan*, ICSID Case No. ARB/12/6, Procedural Order, 3 ICSID 1, 1 (June 12, 2015) (The tribunal ordered the claimant to disclose the identity of the funder. It also ordered disclosure of the 'nature' of the funding arrangement, including the funder's rate of return if the claimant is successful in its claims)
[68] *See ATA Constr., Indus. & Trading Co. v. Hashemite Kingdom of Jordan*, ICSID Case No. ARB/08/02, Order Taking Note of the Discontinuance of the Proceeding 7ICSID (July 11, 2011); *RSM Prod. Corp. v. Grenada*, ICSID Case No. ARB/05/14, Order of the Committee Discontinuing the Proceeding and Decision on Costs, 48 ICSID (Apr. 28, 2011); *Kardassopoulos v. Georgia*, ICSID Case Nos. ARB/05/18 & ARB/07/15, Award, 691 ICSID (Mar. 3, 2010).
[69] Trusz, *supra* note 4, at 1652.
[70] As an example, the UNCITRAL decided three awards (referred to as *Yukos v. The Russian Federation*) in 2014 ordering Russia to pay USD $50 billion. The awards are as follows: *Hulley Enterprises Limited (Cyprus) v. The Russian Federation,* PCA Case No. AA 226, Final Award (July 18, 2014).; *Yukos Universal Limited (Isle of Man) v. The Russian Federation,* PCA Case No. AA 227, Final Award, (July 18, 2014. ; *Veteran Petroleum Limited (Cyprus) v. The Russian Federation,* PCA Case No. AA 228, Final Award (July 18, 2014).

means more complications and more problems.[71] Especially when looking at investor-state arbitration, and particularly cases where the state has lost, taxpayers end up shouldering the burden of the judgment. As such, states have a legitimate interest in making sure that procedures are in place that can limit the possibility of unmeritorious claims being dragged out. Further, the support states can lend to the entire institution of arbitration goes beyond just enforcing judgments, it can help provide binding stop gap measures that increase (to a useful extent) transparency and neutrality in a fairly closed a confidential system.

---

[71] The Notorious B.I.G., *Mo Money Mo Problems,* Life After Death (Bad Boy Records 1997).

[intentionally blank]

[intentionally blank]

[intentionally blank]

THE ARBITRATION BRIEF

Volume 6

The Arbitration Brief is a student publication of American University Washington College of Law prepared with the assistance of the Washington College of Law Center on International Commercial Arbitration. The mission of this publication is to provide timely information, both practical and academic, on developments in the field of arbitration. We welcome pieces from academics, practicing attorneys, arbitrators, and students. For more information, please contact arbitrationbrief@wcl.american.edu. The views expressed in this publication are those of the writers and are not necessarily those of the editors, the Center on International Commercial Arbitration, or American University.

THE ARBITRATION BRIEF STAFF 2019-2020
EDITOR-IN-CHIEF
Michelle Avrutin

MANAGING EDITOR
Leslie Castello

SENIOR ARTICLES EDITORS
Elena Zhilinskaya
Gaensly Joseph

ARTICLES EDITORS
Sabrina Espinal
Marcel Apple
Charles Frazer
Amy Allen
Hannah Stephens
Susan Farhang

www.ingramcontent.com/pod-product-compliance
Lightning Source LLC
Chambersburg PA
CBHW070433220526
45466CB00004B/1664